To Bob Johnson
In the Spirit
of 2 Giants
Harold Washington
+
Martin L King
Words of their Life
Your Pen Has
Touched. Thanks.
for your 40 years
Very Strong.
Rev Al Sampson
1/24/92 Ordained by Dr. Martin L King Jr.

The Black Church and the Harold Washington Story

*The Man

*The Message

*The Movement

Edited with Introduction by Henry J. Young

Mayor
Harold
Washington
(1922-1987)

Wyndham Hall Press

THE BLACK CHURCH
AND THE HAROLD WASHINGTON STORY

Edited with Introduction by
Henry J. Young

Library of Congress Catalog Card Number
88-040117

ISBN 1-55605-045-3

All Rights Reserved

Copyright © 1988 by Henry J. Young

Printed in the United States of America

No portion of this book may be duplicated without the written consent of the author who holds the exclusive copyright. Address inquiries to the publisher, Wyndham Hall Press, Inc., Post Office Box 877, Bristol, IN 46507. U.S.A.

THE HAROLD WASHINGTON STORY

CHURCH GROWTH AND POLITICAL EMPOWERMENT	1
THE SIGNIFICANCE OF HAROLD WASHINGTON
Jeremiah Wright	
FORMATIVE EVENTS IN THE LIFE OF HAROLD WASHINGTON	10
AS TOLD BY A FRIEND
Claude Wyatt	
WHERE DO WE GO FROM HERE?	17
HAROLD WASHINGTON AND THE FUTURE
Eugene Gibson	
THE QUEST FOR UNITY AND IDENTITY IN THE EXPERIENCE OF HAROLD WASHINGTON	23
John Parker	
THE ROLE OF THE DISTRICT SUPERINTENDENT IN THE HAROLD WASHINGTON STORY	30
Charles Wesley Jordan	
THE SPIRITUAL LEGACY OF HAROLD WASHINGTON	35
Wilfred Reid	
HAROLD WASHINGTON AND MARTIN LUTHER KING, JR.	39
NEW FRONTIERS IN CHURCH AND COMMUNITY
Darrell and A. P. Jackson	

NEW DIRECTIONS AND COMMUNITY AND CHURCH DEVELOPMENT 49
THE LEGACY OF HAROLD WASHINGTON
Myron McCoy

TOWARD A MINISTRY OF CARING 54
HAROLD WASHINGTON AND THE FUTURE OF THE BLACK CHURCH
Nathaniel Jarrett

SPIRITUAL FORMATION AND COMMUNITY DEVELOPMENT AS MANIFESTED IN HAROLD WASHINGTON 59
Hycel B. Taylor

THE ROLE OF THE CLERGY IN THE HAROLD WASHINGTON STORY 67
Jesse Cotton

HAROLD WASHINGTON AND THE POLITICS OF INCLUSIVENESS 73
THE BLACK CHURCH THEN AND NOW
Harry B. Gibson

HISTORICAL OVERVIEW OF HAROLD WASHINGTON'S POLITICAL CAREER 80
BEGINNINGS OF "THE MAN-THE MESSAGE-THE MOVEMENT"
John R. Porter

REMEMBERING HAROLD WASHINGTON 89
Eddie L. Robinson

THE ROLE OF WOMEN IN THE HAROLD
WASHINGTON STORY   95
Addie Wyatt

THE BLACK CHURCH AND THE POLITICS OF
LIBERATION AS REFLECTED IN THE HAROLD
WASHINGTON STORY   104
George W. Walker

THE BLACK CHURCH AS AGENT OF SOCIAL
CHANGE   109
THE HAROLD WASHINGTON STORY
Willie Barrow

REFLECTIONS ON HAROLD WASHINGTON AS A
SYMBOL OF UNITY IN THE LIFE OF THE CHURCH
AND THE BLACK COMMUNITY   114
Marvell Williams
Charles Murray
Willie L. Upshire
Clay Evans

THE IMPORTANCE OF THE BLACK CHURCH AND
COMMUNITY ORGANIZATION IN THE HAROLD
WASHINGTON STORY   121
Al Sampson

HAROLD WASHINGTON   126
A CALL TO ECONOMIC DEVELOPMENT
George Reddick

HAROLD WASHINGTON   134
A CHAMPION OF HOPE
Sylvester Brinson, III

BLACK EVANGELICALISM AND THE POLITICAL PROCESS AS REFLECTED IN THE HAROLD WASHINGTON STORY   140
Clarence Hilliard

THE SIGNIFICANCE OF THE HAROLD WASHINGTON STORY FOR BLACK WOMEN IN MINISTRY   144
Brenda Little

HAROLD WASHINGTON AS A ROLE MODEL FOR BLACK YOUTH   149
D. C. Coleman

HAROLD WASHINGTON DEMONSTRATED THAT "IT CAN BE DONE"   153
Henry Hardy

HAROLD WASHINGTON AND THE VALUE OF CHURCH AND COMMUNITY DEVELOPMENT   157
Carroll Felton, Jr.

EULOGY OF MAYOR HAROLD WASHINGTON   167
B. Herbert Martin

NOTES ON CONTRIBUTORS   176

ACKNOWLEDGEMENTS

Many persons contributed to the birth of this project. The project was conceived originally when B. Herbert Martin delivered the Eulogy of Harold Washington. When I listened to how B. Herbert made an acute connection between *The Black Church and the Harold Washington Story*, I realized suddenly that there needed to be a volume to demonstrate this point. I thought it was important to do this because of its historic and contemporary significance in the life of the black church and the black community. Therefore, it is important to begin with expressing a deep appreciation to B. Herbert Martin and his role as pastor of Harold Washington.

When I decided to pursue this idea, the first persons which I contacted were Carroll Felton, Jr., Myron McCoy, Harry B. Gibson and Al Sampson. I called them together to serve in an advisory capacity. Other persons which joined, in this regard, were Eddie Robinson and Henry Hardy. The advisory helped to identify and select the persons represented in this volume. I am indeed appreciative of their hard work. It is important to note, however, that many persons that should be included in this volume are not represented because of space and time limitations. The persons represented here are meant to be illustrative; they are not meant to be exhaustive of all persons that deserve representation.

The offices of The Vice President for Academic Affairs and The Church and The Black Experience of Garrett-Evangelical Theological Seminary contributed financially to this project. Funds were provided to assist in the purchasing of tapes. Also, funds were provided to assist in the transcription of interview tapes. The Council on Ministries of the Northern Illinois, United Methodist Church, helped financially with the transcription of taped interviews.

Sherri Young, administrative assistant in the office of student affairs at Garrett-Evangelical Theological Seminary, assisted with the transcription of interview tapes. Other persons assisting were Emily Townes, a doctoral student in ethics and society in the joint Garrett-Northwestern Graduate Program, Joyce Parks, Legal Secretary for the Mayor, Brown Platt firm, Joyce Cassells and Claudia Moore. Each worked untiringly for many hours to get the tapes transcribed. And, Linda Koops, who serves as a faculty secretary at Garrett-Evangelical Theological Seminary, assisted in printing the entire manuscript after it was transcribed.

Many thanks are be given to my wife, Aleta Joyce and daughter, Aleta Renee, for their toleration of the many hours which I spent with this project. For their support and understanding I will always be grateful.

INTRODUCTION: A REVIEW OF THE LITERATURE

Henry James Young

The purpose of this volume is to illustrate, through *The Harold Washington Story*, the contention that the black church is the vanguard of social activism in the black community. I argued earlier, employing key religious figures as examples, that the black church has always been on the cutting edge of social, political and economic development in the black community. This thesis was developed in two volumes, *Major Black Religious Leaders: 1755-1940* and *Major Black Religious Leaders: 1940 to the Present*. Both were published by Abingdon Press, Nashville, Tennessee. The present volume attempts to illustrate how the black church pioneered in making *The Harold Washington Story* possible, in terms of Harold's success as Mayor of the city of Chicago. It is a contemporary case study demonstrating a truth which has been affirmed for a long time by many scholars in religious studies.

Not only has it been a long standing accepted truth by scholars in religious studies that the black church is the only social institution which is owned and controlled by the black community; but it has always served as an agent of social change within the community. The dominant and prevailing theological orientation within the black church is not one geared toward an otherworldly eschatological hope. By this mean a hope that is focused almost exclusively toward life after death. Rather, the prevailing theological orientation within the black church is consistent in integrating spirituality and social transformation. In other words, it tends to combine Christian hope with impacting social change within society. We can find this truth illustrated by several scholars in religious studies.

For example, the noted sociologist, E. Franklin Frazier in his book, entitled, *The Negro Church in America*, shows that in the early formation of the black church, its significance resided in providing social cohesiveness for the black community. Although Frazier does spend some time discussing those aspects of black religion, during the modern institution of slavery, which tended to emphasize a type of otherworldly eschatological hope, his man contribution attempts to show how the black church pioneered in impacting socio-economic structures. Carter G. Woodson in his book on *The Negro Church* spends considerably time tracing the development of various historic black congregations and their impact on the social environment. Benjamin Quarles in his book *The Negro in the Making of America*, indicates an abiding appreciation for the black church and its historic role in generating social change within the environment. The early study made by Benjamin Elijah Mays and Nicholson entitled, *The Negro Church*, is helpful in showing how the black church served historically as a catalyst of social and psychological identity within the black community. In other words, during the era of segregation and political disenfranchisement when every effort was being made by the majority social group in America to reduce black men and women to a level of depersonalization, Mays and Nicholson show how the black church enabled them to discover a source of identity.

The book entitled, *The Negro's God*, by Benjamin E. Mays is important in that it shows the religious and social dimensions of the black church. Mays helps us to see that the theological orientation within the black church has always had a particular socio-cultural context. And, the social context has always been focused around modifying environmental conditions. This is illustrated by Howard Thurman in his book, *Jesus and the Disinherited*. Also, we can find developed in W.E.B. DuBois' classic study, *The Souls of Black Folk*.

Some more contemporary discussions related to the thesis developed in this volume can be found in the following: Martin Luther King, Jr.'s books, *Where Do We Go From Here: Chaos or Community?, Pilgrimage to Nonviolence, Strength to Love,* and *Trument of Conscience,* all attest to the fact that the black church was integral to the whole Civil Rights Movement in America. James H. Cone appeals to the black church to become more involved in the struggle for liberation in his first book, *Black Theology and Black Power.* He developed his radical stance in some of his later works such as *A Black Theology of Liberation.* In his book *Spirituals and the Blues,* James Cone attempts to affirm the social radicalism which he perceived to be present in the historic development of black religion. And, in this regard, it is important to mention Howard Thurman's two volumes on the Negro Spirituals, *Deep River,* and *The Negro Spiritual Speaks of Life and Death.* Both are illustrative of the spiritual and social dimensions of the black religious experience.

In James Cone's book, *God of the Oppressed,* there is a strong affirmation of the black church and its significance in impacting social change in the environment. He continues this theme in his latest book, *For My People.* Alongside of James H. Cone is another important contributor to the black theology discussion. His name is James Deotis Roberts. Both James H. Cone and J. Deotis Roberts pioneered in the development of black theology.

The first major book by J. Deotis Roberts, which launched his program of black theology focused on liberation and reconciliation. In his *Black Theology and Reconciliation,* J. Deotis attempted to create an alternative to James H. Cone's perspective. The fundamental difference between the two reside in their understanding of liberation. For James H. Cone liberation focuses on blackness as an ontological symbol, meaning that the liberation activity for the oppressed both begins and ends with "blackness." In other words, for Cone whites have to integrate blackness existentially as an ontological symbol at the level of consciousness raising in order to participate fully in the quest for liberation and reconciliation. Whereas, for J. Deotis Roberts, the point of departure for liberation remains an open ended agenda. For him no one particular ethnic social group determines its beginning and ending.

In his book, *A Black Political Theology*, J. Deotis Roberts attempts to show how the black community must integrate the spiritual and political dimensions of the Gospel of Christ into its foundations. He attempts to provide an agenda for integrating the political dimension into the quest for liberation and reconciliation. His latest book published by Westminster Press, deals with *Black Theology in Dialogue with Third World Theologies*. His contention is that black theology must begin to create a meaningful dialogue with other similar emerging theologies.

C. Eric Lincoln's book entitled, *The Black Church Since Frazier*, is important in that it shows how the black church has advanced subsequent to the time of slavery and reconstruction. In other words, Lincoln argues that there is a fundamental difference between The Negro Church, which E. Franklin Frazier described and The Black Church which emerged during the Black Power era in the 1960s. His thesis is that the Negro Church tended to be rather conservative and the Black Church is radical and militant. Another important book published by Lincoln besides his monumental study of *The Black Muslims in America*, is his volume dealing with *Race, Religion, and the Continuing American Dilemma*. In this volume Lincoln shows how the problem of institutional racism continues to militate against the possibility for genuine social pluralism to be realized in the American society.

The particular orientation which Lincoln provides in *The Black Church Since Frazier* is also developed in Gayraud Wilmore's book, *The Black Religion and Radicalism*. Wilmore argues that the post-reconstruction black church became reactionary and conservative. Wilmore challenges the present black church to rediscover its historic roots of involvement into social, political and economic activism.

Works that give a more philosophical orientation to the quest for liberation in the black community are provided by William Jones of Florida State University and Cornel West of Union Theological Seminary, New York City. Jones' book, *Is God a White Racist?*, attempts to raise major questions to black theologians about the problem of black suffering, on the one hand, and, their affirmation of a just and loving God, on the other hand. His contention is that black theologians need to resolve this dilemma before any meaningful program of black theology can be developed.

Cornel West in his book, *Prophecy and Deliverance*, provides an insightful appraisal of black religion employing categories from the Marxist perspective. His effort is to discover what is most viable in black religion, which is applicable for liberation.

There is a need to mention the book which was recently released by Mercer University Press, Macon, Georgia entitled, *The Color of God* by Major J. Jones, who is presently serving as chaplain of the Atlanta University Center, Atlanta, Georgia. Jones' book is important in that it provides a helpful review of existing literature in black theology. It is useful in introducing persons to the discussion of black theology, in terms of the major interpreters.

So, then, I have provided this rather brief discussion of selected literature in the development of the black church to illustrate how there is an acute connection between *The Harold Washington Story* and the historic mission and ministry of the black.

This volume contains chapters by some of the key leaders in the Harold Washington political campaign. Many clergy represented in this volume were with Harold Washington from the very inception of the movement to his recent death. Not only were they the interpreters of the movement, in terms of the interrelatedness to the black church, but they were among the ones that pioneered in making the movement happen. Based on the insights contained in the narratives disclosed here it is my hope that the black church at large will use them as a basis to facilitate its social sensitivity.

CHURCH GROWTH AND POLITICAL EMPOWERMENT

THE SIGNIFICANCE OF HAROLD WASHINGTON

Jeremiah Wright

My involvement in the political career of Harold Washington goes back to when he was in the Congress. I was a member of his educational task force and was sent, prior to being put on that task force, a long list of questions about educational reform. When he started to run for mayor of Chicago I was working with a group of ministers, a coalition which included Claude Wyatt, Jesse Cotton, D. C. Coleman, Gregory Ingram and Nathaniel Jarrett. The coalition was referred to as clergy for Harold Washington. My mechanical and ministerial involvement was as follows: The clergy coalition took out a full page ad in the paper. I worded the ad that went in the paper. Jesse Cotton, I think, was the convenor of our committee meeting.

The ad pointed out that the undersigned clergy were endorsing Harold Washington. We endorsed him as individual clergy persons, because a church cannot endorse a candidate. We believed that he was qualified; we believed he was an excellent statesman; and we believed he was honest and sincere about political reform. We pledged all of our support to work as hard as we could to get him elected. We wanted to hold him accountable to the black community. We promised him that if he reneged on his promises and if we found him to be just another old politician in the Chicago mold, we would work just as hard to get him unelected. He appreciated the honesty. He also appreciated our candor.

Then after that, I had him here at the church for a couple of rallies where he came in as a candidate in the afternoon; he had specially prepared political forums to speak before the first election. During the second election, he came in during his term for a State of the Race Seminar with an all day workshop. He spoke from a political point of view.

I preached vociferously for several sermons not only in Trinity United Church of Christ, but throughout the city of Chicago about the importance of Harold Washington's election. I was targeting two groups, the eighteen year old young adults and the persons within the black community that lacked self confidence about the Harold Washington campaign. I wanted to get them to believe in themselves so that they could go home, for example, and talk about the significance of the Harold Washington campaign, as they would talk about Michael Jackson, Luther Vandross, Anita Baker, and so forth. This is important because there is a lot of lack of self esteem among some of their parents. Also, this problem is found among some of our own church members. I found myself having to constantly fight against the lack of self esteem in the black community.

I preached several sermons about the lack of self esteem in the black community, as it relates to every fact of the black experience. I was quite critical of the prevailing mentality which says that anything the white community says is right; in other words, many contend that as long as it is from the white community, it is better than what is to be found in the black community. Because of this I lost several members of Trinity United Church of Christ to the Apostolic faith. They went to the Apostolic faith because they believed we were too politically oriented in the first Harold Washington campaign. I was actively involved in the campaign at every level in both the first and second election.

In fact, one of the former members that left and went to the Apostolic faith called Dr. Gardner Taylor, who is senior minister of the Concord Baptist Church in New York City. The person called

Gardner Taylor because Gardner had preached at the Apostolic Church recently. The person told Gardner Taylor that Trinity United Church of Christ had split. Gardner asked, "Well how many members have gone to the Apostolic faith?" After discovering that only twelve members had gone, Gardner said, "Well the Trinity United Church of Christ I know, that's not even worthy of being considered a splinter, let along a split."

Why does this happen? I think it happens because many of our new members do not come in with a sense of history about where we have been as a people and as a congregation. They are not aware of the decision we made to be a church that is unashamedly black and unapologetically Christian. The fact that we decided to be a church in 1981, to adopt a black value system is all new to them. It is alien to them. So I am starting with square one with a lot of new members. We have to bring them into a level of consciousness about the road over which we have come and the way which we have decided to be as a people of faith covenanted together. This is an ongoing process.

Harold Washington appointed me to the City College Board, while he was in office. My work with the political process says something about my conception of ministry. In 1980, I led the congregation of Trinity United Church of Christ into the development of a ten point vision for the eighties for our church. The church is implementing two of the principles each year. One of the principles is to have a politically aware congregation. Now, what does it mean to be politically aware? It begins with consciousness raising.

When I come down hard in my sermons, in terms of the recognition that we are made in the image of God, male and female, I help them to understand how God's creativity contains implications for political development. For example, we are created in God's image with our black skin and thick lips and curly hair; it means that we should possess high self esteem. The recognition that one is created in the image and likeness of God is the highest expression of self esteem that I can think of. It means empowerment. To have low self esteem is to distort the image of God.

How are you going to read Mary's Magnifica or Hannah's prayer and not see the political implication of that, in terms of the world in which we live? So the answer is yes, the political dimension is a very definite part of ministry. For example, St. John 1:1, "In the beginning was the word, and the word was with God." Everyone loves the poetry and it sounds great in King James, But the word became flesh and dwelled among us. This has implications socially, politically, economically, culturally, as well as spiritually. It relates to everything that we do. It is a manifestation of incarnational theology.

But the question many will ask is whether my direct involvement in the political process is related to the rapid growth of Trinity United Church of Christ? I have had to tell this story over and over again across the country. The fact is that Trinity United Church of Christ has been acclaimed several times by the United Church of Christ denomination that it is the fastest growing congregation in the denomination. Also, it is acclaimed as the largest congregation in the denomination.

And wherever I tell the story one of the things that I point out is that if the pastor doesn't have the congregation's approval, permission and backing in implementing programs, he/she is fighting a losing battle. The congregation made a decision prior to my coming as paster. That was one of the biggest assets which I had, in terms of helping me bring people together. The congregation made a decision in 1971, that it was a white church in black faith. At the time, the congregation was ten years old and like many other mainline predominately black congregations, it was having a severe identity crisis.

Most of the mainline denominations when they started a congregation for blacks, whether it was in a changing neighborhood or a new situation, unfortunately and tragically, the notion was never geared toward all kinds of people; rather, it was focused on a certain type of people. What happened as the result of the congregational missionaries setting up schools for the freedmen who taught blacks reading, writing, history, mathematics, etiquette and so forth, they also taught blacks New England worship styles. Being missionaries they educated blacks away from their own culture and identity. Not only was this the case in education, but also, in terms of the belief that "this is the way one worships God, aright" (to use a New England word).

One of the four predecessor churches, said we needed a church for the graduates of our American Missionary Association (AMA) schools, because they were believed to be a cut above the ordinary black person. Well, they tried on in the 1890s; but it failed. They tried another one in 1909, and named it in honor of Lincoln. It still exists as the oldest black college.

So in 1931, you get a Congregational Christian Church that merges and then in 1957, we became the United Church of Christ. Now that United Church of Christ wants a church for the single-family, home owning persons moving into this neighborhood, not Princeton Park tenement people or project people. And this is what we have. We started that way and we grew under two pastors. But then in the lat 1960s, the black revolution hit; the black consciousness movement hit, black gospel music began being sung on black college campuses, and folks started saying no, wait a minute.

The missionaries are wrong. We don't have to give up who we are to be educated. As a result, our church membership went down to eighty seven members. The congregation decided a difficult question before they called anybody: Are we going to be a black church in a black community or are we going to be a white church in black face? Because in 1971, all we had in our church outside of Sunday morning services and church school was a yoga class in the middle of the week. We had no Bible study; we had no social programs relating to anything in this community. So they made a decision and wrote up an understanding of who they are and where they wanted to go.

They showed it to the candidates who were applying for the pastorate. So that's a very important point. The congregation made a decision prior to calling a new pastor. So when they showed me their decision and asked if I could help them become a black church, I laughed and said, "it is like throwing a rabbit in a briar patch. Come on. Let's go and let's have some fun." In March of 1971, I started and entered in a covenant. As a matter of fact, we used a portion of their statement during the ordination service where we covenanted together to work in this new direction. And, in many ways, when I look back 16 years ago at getting on my horse and taking off in all different directions at once, the teenagers were very significant in those years.

They did for us here, at this congregation, what the students at Howard University did in 1968, when they formed a Gospel Choir. The kids here wanted a choir. After they had a few rehearsals, the president called me and said, "Reverend Wright, this is not what we meant. We want to sing black music." And the musician was not teaching them black music. So they hired a nineteen year old high school graduate, by the name of Jeffrey Radford. He was in College at that time. Presently, he serves as the Minister of Music. That choir began singing in October of 1971. We have a plaque on the wall from that first Sunday they sang here at Trinity. This event took place on the fifth Sunday in October, 1972. It was called the Youth Fellowship Choir.

Adults came to me complaining that they wanted to get in the choir. We were calling it the Youth Fellowship Choir for Schoolers. We changed the name to the Trinity Choral Ensemble in 1973, and adults got into it. And that music program became a significant piece in attracting worshippers to the church. The first year I was here, we took in sixty new members. Our budget then was thirty-four thousand dollars. The next year, we took in eighty-three new members; in 1971, we took in seventy-six new members;

in 1975-79, it was always over one hundred to one hundred and forty. But in 1979, when we went on the radio we went off the charts, in terms of quantum leaps. There had not bee a year since 1979 where was have taken in less than four hundred new members per year. This is due primarily to the radio medium. We ask new members how did they hear about the church and the answer is usually the radio.

It is the radio ministry that has pulled new members from all over the city. When I conduct training workshops on Evangelism, I always point out worship is the key. Worship is the key in attracting new members. One of the things we did, in terms of relating to the community, immediately in 1973, we began the planning process an din 1974, we started implementing the plan.

We have a federally funded Title 20 program for unemployed, underemployed, welfare parents, families, and so forth. It is open from 7:00 a.m. to 6:00 p.m., twelve months a year. The teachers have college degrees; some have graduate degrees. Now, within a fourteen year time period not one of those parents taking advantage of our services have joined the church. Because that is not why people join the church. They don't joint the church because of our daycare program. We have a Headstart program; they don't join church because of the feeding program. We have a tutorial program; that is not why people join the church.

The social services of the church and the ministries of the church are very important and valuable; but that is not what makes people join. So that the worship attracts them. We have found that the educational program, the program of ministry and service, the combination of head and heart, the social action piece, and others are what keeps them here. But that's not why they came. They join because of the same old Biblical witness. Be my witness. Peter standing up saying what must we do to be saved? That's why they're at the church. That's why they become members of the church. I've said to my musicians, and we have a staff of twenty-five now, that quality in worship is the key of effectiveness in church growth. But this means preparation. Prepare your services well, including your order of worship, songs, hymns, and so forth. For example, one should preach as if it's the last time the Lord is going to allow one to preach. You should do the very best that you can do that day. One of the things that kills churches is the whole attitude among the clergy, "that will do it, I'll do better next week." God might not give you another chance; and if every time we stand up to lead in worship, whether it's music and/or ministry of the spoken word, we should do our best.

Now, how many members do we have? We only count active dues payers. My father used to tell me if you ask the average black pastor what is his/her membership, whatever the figure is the preachers gives you, you can always divide by two and sometimes three. So we have been very conscious across the years of cleaning the rolls of persons who have moved, changed membership, and just haven't let us know. We monitor it by the giving records and the activity records. When they fill out their pledge cards, in terms of what they're going to tithe or give; they also indicate where they're going to work in the church; so they become an active part of the ministry of the church. And Bible study, we check the Bible study rolls to see how many are enrolled. Weekly we have anywhere from 15-20 adult Bible class offerings. We look for each trimester of the year to see what Bible courses people took to determine whether they are active. We are aware that everybody don't make money and some can't give.

We've got over five hundred unemployed people. So the rolls, in terms of our giving units right now reflect over four thousand and six hundred giving units. We're not talking about any silk stockings here; we've talking poor folks. We are talking about a complete mixed bag, because one of the things we have pushed across the years, in terms of what it means to be a black church, is that what we calls ourselves affectionately and affirm the fact that we are an alphabet soup. We have all persons represented in our congregation.

Now, as we think about the significant role the black church played in the Harold Washington campaign, its value cannot be measured. Harold Washington was a breath of fresh air to the black church at large. He was a product of the black church. One place to measure his value resides in role modeling. He was indeed a positive role model for all oppressed persons. Because it does pay for us to push our youth toward positive role models. Harold Washington represented a symbol of what is possible. We must teach our youth that they might not have the capacity to be a Michael Jordan, Walter Payton or Douglas Williams, but they all can learn to read and write. They can learn to be excellent in all that they do.

FORMATIVE EVENTS IN THE LIFE OF HAROLD WASHINGTON

AS TOLD BY A FRIEND

Claude Wyatt

My relationship with Harold Washington goes back a long ways. I met Harold when we were in school together; we were in several classes together at DuSable High School. I graduated in 1940, and Harold came out just a semester after I did. But, I used to see him around the gym. In fact, I teased him about how I used to look over his shoulder when we would have a test in Civics class.

There were three things that stood out about Harold Washington when we were at DuSable High School. First, he was a brilliant student. He always passed his tests and he was a very studious kind of guy. Secondly, he always used to hang around the gymnasium all the time. He enjoyed swimming and he played a little basketball. I didn't play too much basketball but I tried to do some swimming. The third thing about Harold Washington is that he was a very, very sociable guy. Everybody knew him around school. Every time you saw him he would be laughing; he was in ROTC, and I think he tried to play a little football too.

During my experience at DuSable High School, I had no idea of becoming a minister. I saw Harold as a very studious person and I never thought in terms of him becoming a lawyer. As a matter of fact, my mentality at that time wasn't of such. All we could do was think about getting out of school and perhaps getting a job so we could make some money, because we were all poor. However, Harold always seemed to be a little bit on the upper economic ladder. His family had a little more money that most of us did; he functioned very well around school, socially as well as being a rather prominent person. Of course, we just went to school and after school we would get little jobs on the street someplace, but Harold was never found in those areas; there was a difference in our economic conditions.

Being in the community, I ran into Harold Washington quite frequently. But later on, as he began to become a little more prominent in the ward he was working in, then I think we began to establish a more substantive relationship; because we became involved with the union at that time and it certainly did have some drawing relationships for us. My wife, Addie Wyatt, was working with the union at 48th and Wabash and, of course, that threw us right into the sixth ward with Ralph Metcalf; and we were able to work with people like Ralph, Harold and others. That was another establishing point for our relationship. Also, working with my wife in the union brought me in contact with Martin Luther King, Jr.

When I first met King, I was in and out of school and working at the post office trying to support my family; my wife was working at the union at that time, United Packinghouse Workers at 48th and Wabash. I was often involved in different programs, offering invocations, sometimes just to be there and going to dinners, and so forth. They made a plan to bring Dr. King to Chicago after he became popular from the boycotts; so I took off from work one Wednesday, back in 1967, and I went down to the Pick-Congress Hotel. They had a big luncheon for him and it was there that I first met him. He was a very impressive person. The moment I saw him, he gripped me. He was very friendly and very warm. He just seemed to impress me in a sense. I just couldn't walk away from him, I had to come back and talk to him again. And after talking with him, he promised Charlie Hayes, who was the director at the union, that he would come back and work with us. I followed his career in the newspapers and he constantly stayed in touch with Charlie Hayes. My wife was Program Coordinator, so whenever the union sponsored a program involving Dr. King, she had to be in touch with him. So, through that kind of relationship, I got to know him; and when he came to Chicago the next time, we were meeting with a group of leaders and I was invited to the dinner to give the invocation again. As a matter of act, I was sitting next to Dr. King. So out of that came a very good relationship of working with Dr. King. Then one day he came to us and he said he was going to send a young man into Chicago. He said: I want you to work with him and to take care of him for me. He's a good man and I know that you, Charlie, Addie, and others are going to do a good job for me. So just take care of this young man, because he's really going to be a success. We said, "Okay, fine. Bring him in." We were all at an NAACP meeting (Rev. Willie Barrow was my assistant at that time in community relations) and they brought Jesse Jackson in. Jesse was about 23 years old at the time. I think we met at Clay Evans church. Several of us got together and acquired an apartment for Jesse Jackson; we signed for the apartment. From that point, we began to work in the community and then Harold Washington, I think, became alderman at that time, and we began to work closely with him. If Harold Washington was trying to do something in the community and we knew about it, then we were there to support him.

Well, to be very frank, when Harold Washington first made his first trial run in the 70s, I met with him and a group of ministers and decided to support him in that effort. It was a trial run and we think he did very well at that time. Then later on, Harold didn't rally want to run for office, and he sort of got shipped away to Washington, D.C. as a congressman, but we kept in touch with him. He set up a ministerial group here in Chicago and constantly met with us, dealing with problems in the community and sharing some of his congressional concerns. Most of them dealt with registration; many times it was housing and things like that. We worked with him in the community. Both Harold Washington and Martin Luther King, Jr., were concerned with housing.

Harold Washington wasn't a Johnny-come-lately. No, no. Harold was right there on the scene. Of course, he wasn't always around

Chicago, and he wasn't at every meeting; but at all the significant meetings, he was there.

The significant thing about Harold Washington's campaign wasn't so much the message as it was the man. You see, everybody was saying what Harold Washington was saying; and Harold Washington was saying what everybody else had said. He was just a little more articulate. It was the strength of Harold Washington that made the difference. He was a man who had fortitude and strength. He was fearless. It didn't make any difference who you were, if you were wrong, he would tell you. He would stand toe-to-toe, face-to-face and he wasn't embarrassed to tell you who you were and who he was. He was quite confident about himself; he was sure; he knew he had things going for himself. Harold was just a power of strength to that extent. That was the thing that really just gave Harold the image in the community; because he would just stand tip-toe and talk with you. And then, he didn't try to throw off a lot of educational stuff on you, a lot of law and all that king of thing. He just kind of "shot from the hip," so to speak, and what he said made sense. And he made it real clear and plain, in terms of what he stood for, what he was doing, and what he wanted you to do. And he didn't mind calling shots.

Well, he was an intelligent guy and he was brainy. Harold was no pushover. He could stand on his feet and out-think you in a minute. I used to tease him all the time. "Harold," I said, "you've as dangerous as a pocket full of loose razor blades. You can laugh and smile at a person, and win them, and you're cutting them to shreds at the same time."

Harold was the people's choice for Mayor. But I don't think he was the people's choice, in terms of the movement. I think he played a significant role in the movement, in terms of a lawyer and as a person, but I don't think he was the people's choice altogether in terms of that. I think what really happened is that Harold was so self-confident that he didn't push himself to do things. If he wanted to do something, he could get it done. They begged him to run for mayor the first time and he said, "No, I don't want to run." And they begged, and begged, and begged, and he finally said, "Okay, I'll try it." So he threw his hat out there to get the feel of it. The second time, they begged him again and again, he said no. He was happy with his congressional seat. And he was just a guy like that. He was doing a good job in Washington and the congressional fellows there didn't want him to leave. They wanted him to stay there. But we worked on him a little bit and he said, "Well, maybe I'll take a look at it." He thought it over and he came in. Harold was in and out of Chicago all the time and knew what was doing on. Harold was no dummy at all.

In my own case, I know I had some very serious political problems at our church, and our foundation laid there for seven years. No bank would touch us. A lot of things happened to us there. We spent a lot of money. We were in court every month for seven years, up until 1985. That happened back in 1978. After Harold was elected, we went downtown to talk with him about it. He said to let him review the case and he turned it over to the attorney. The attorney reviewed the case and saw nothing wrong. He asked, "Do you have the money to build?" We said yet, and brought the statements. I had my lawyer draw up all the financial papers and he went down to talk with the head counsel there and they said, "Well, we see no reasons why you can't build -- you've got the money. What about your plans?" I said that the plans were on hold now. They said to complete your plans and get them ready. We see no reason for delay and they released me from the courts. It was just a question of having the plans certified. So my contractor went down and had the plans certified. That was in 1984 -- 1985 we were in the church; but for seven years it sat there. The election of Harold Washington made the difference.

Harold was a very kind person and I think he was people-oriented to that extent. The things that happened to people concerned him and he would get angry. Many times in places he would get angry and say "I don't have to take that stuff off of them!" He was just a person who was not afraid. He was quite sure of himself. He had his homework done. He knew what was legal; he knew what to do. You might just say "the guy had guts," and that pushed him on through.

Now, where do we go from here? Harold Washington is now dead and what's the future for Chicago!

Well, I think the first step, is the need to come together. This city has been torn apart by leaders in the community, not having an understanding. I think in a sense there might have been some selfishness, but we need to come together because before we can move forward, we have to get our things together here. The other thing is that, a we look at the community, I think it's very important that we begin to build a coalition. I don't think we can just stand around until some guy comes out of school, or out of a law office and decides he or she wants to run for office without knowing what Chicago is all about. Some person jumps out of a big corporation and somebody wants to put him or her in because they think he or she is a brilliant person and has a law background, but the person normally doesn't understand the problems of the welfare mother. I think we need a coalition now where we can sit down and begin to hand down and to hand up. If you're sitting up there, then send something down, and when you come down here I'll push something up to you. We will let you know what's going on down here and vice versa. I think i the Black community we need that kind of a close coalition. There are no heroes. Many people might want to be or try to be, but there are no heroes. Because if I fail, then all fail. If they fail, I fail. We've all Black people and its for our Black community and it must be cemented together -- not because of who's the most popular or who can speak the loudest or anything like that -- but it must be because of the fact that we are all tuned in on one thing; and that's building community through coalition. I think that's very, very important.

The other thing is that we can no longer allow ourselves to be concerned with driving our Mercedes and things like that. People should be able to enjoy those things, but when you look around and see what's going on in the community with our young people -- they've lost just about everything. They don't have very many images now. They don't have to live up to what White folks say about them. The don't have to take every habit off the TV, every style off the TV, walking around with boots and a big wide hat and most of them have never been out of Chicago. What do they know about mountains and Western styles. But they pick up every style that comes out of Hollywood and New York. They want to be that and what it is doing is damning the mind. And the minds are being darkened and we have a responsibility to get hold of these young minds; and we have a responsibility to pry open their minds and put something in them. It cannot be done if they see confusion and strife among the leaders. Church leaders, political leaders, community leaders -- we cannot be a team if they go home and find daddy and momma fussing, fighting, drinking cussing, shooting dope, and all that kind of stuff. We've got to do something about that. And that's one of my deep concerns.

I think (1) there has to be a better economic base for all the people, (2) there must be some decent housing in decent neighborhoods for everyone, and (3) education. I don't mean necessarily that everyone has to go to a university, but there has to be education in the community where people can upgrade themselves. I'm not against Bible teaching, because we all teach that. Teach the Bible and I'm really for that. I think that's a basic. But we've got to take that Bible and we've got to break that down so that people can understand what the Bible is saying to them here and now, rather than there and then. And that's very important at this point. Most people come to church and we clap our hands and we have a good time and we enjoy it. But we need to have a better understanding of what God is all about in light of the needs of the community.

WHERE DO WE GO FROM HERE?

HAROLD WASHINGTON AND THE FUTURE

Eugene Gibson

I've been involved in the Black Church and the Political Process of Black Politics in Chicago for a long time. In fact, I was born in Chicago at Cook County Hospital. Prior to the Harold Washington situation, there was the Mayor Daley era, which lasted for over twenty years. During this time, Black aldermen were not empowered. Many of them were just there to fill a seat, were some of the White alderman. So consequently, when Harold Washington first put his name on the ballot in the late 70s, it represented the beginning of hope for oppressed persons.

Harold Washington was an eloquent speaker. He was quite accomplished in his communication skills. Harold did it second to none. I became interested. Some of my brothers called me because I had been President of the Roseland Church Association. They knew how I felt about social action and the political process. So they called me and said, "Harold Washington is serious and he's not going to run until he knows he has somebody behind him." So I talked to the men and women that are affiliated with the Roseland Church Association. The number consisted of over 50 persons. They appeared to be serious; some were a little reluctant. But many though, of course, that the Jane Byrne situation would come up again. They believed that she would get back in office again. So they were a little bit afraid. The alderman in this were demonstrating loyalty to Jane Byrne, so therefore, guys felt that they had to be very careful about endorsing Harold Washington. So, I talked to a woman friend of mine who I've been knowing for years. Her husband was a great preacher in this city and she (Elva

Bailey) called me and said, "Gene, Harold Washington is the ideal candidate for the city of Chicago. I said, "great." She replied, "Can he come by the church?" I said, "yes, bring him by the church," because he actually had to look for churches that people would let him come in and speak. People were a little bit afraid. I said "bring Harold by. She said, "great." He came by on a Sunday morning and just had a fantastic time here at the church. New Reporters from Channel 5 were here with him. The fact is that we all had a great time. The way he was able to relate to the members of this church was outstanding. He had a very humble attitude; it wasn't flashy. He said, "I'm for the people." He reminded me of Martin Luther King, Jr. Many times, black brethren or sisters that can speak eloquently find themselves becoming too grandiose. Harold Washington was in the caliber of Martin Luther King, Jr. He was prepared. In my opinion, he was the ideal candidate. So immediately, I shared this with my congregation. And normally, I do not endorse candidate for political office. My endorsement of Harold Washington was the second time that I endorsed anyone for political office. I endorsed Howard Brookings who was a member of this church. I baptized him. I endorsed him and I endorsed Harold Washington. I never endorsed any other candidate. Immediately, I encouraged some of my members to become a part of the voter registration drive, I took about fifteen of my members downtown and had them register as voter registrars.

I actually encourage the Roseland Church Association members to do the same thing; because of that, we had from this area over eighty voter registrars. They endorsed Harold Washington and got people to register to vote.

And then, we moved along from that particular point. We organized meetings, worked, prayed, caucused, and raised funds. And we were a little afraid because we had to deal with the separation between church and state. We were threatened with that principle, but we decided to face the consequences. So consequently, we raised our monies, and, of course, Harold Washington won.

Immediately after Harold's victory, the ministers did not want to break up so we formed the Chicago Black Clergy. We elected Jesse Cotton to be our president, and Jesse did a fantastic job. In fact, I was elected one of the vice presidents, along with Henry Hardy, Claude Wyatt and Harry Gibson. I was one in charge of the spiritual aspect. It was the first time that the clergy from the west side and the south side came together. In the past there was always a separation. The Dan Ryan expressway separated us; it was the dividing wall between the west side and the south side. Other factors contributed to this separation as well. But we came together, and it was a coalition of west side as well as south side ministers that formed the Black Clergy. It was ecumenical and Interdenominational. We got along well, like brothers and sisters.

From that, of course, came the second election with the voter registration, and so forth. From that particular coalition, I moved into the area of ethics. Jesse Cotton, along with a couple ministers and myself, served on the Steering Committee that was shared by Done Benedict to construct an ethics ordinance that was submitted to the City Council. We spend about two years, meeting twice downtown a month for two years. Rev. Basil Foley, Rev. Nathaniel Jarrett, Rev. Jesse Cotton, along with myself and a couple of aldermen (Orr and others) -- it was a blue ribbon committee. Finally, we were able to bring that to the City Council. But because of controversy in the council, the ethics ordinance was battered back and forth for almost a year. This suggested that the ministers finally had real input now in City Hall. They had input because of their work, and camaraderie which was beginning to exist between the ministers and themselves (south side and west side). Also, we realized that we had a common cause. We knew now that we did not have to go down to City Hall and take second place. We knew that we didn't have to plow anymore, we could preach. So therefore, it brought a sense of pride, a sense of togetherness. We lost a sense of hopelessness and were able to put on an air of belonging, partnership and ownership in the City; we had not been able to do this all of our lives. I was born in this City fifty-two years ago. In the past we were not able to do what the Harold Washington era permitted.

Prior to Harold Washington, the frustration that you would experience going down to City Hall not knowing who to talk to and not seeing a Black face, was a problem that concerned us. Those days were over. Those days were over. The day of having to vote or speak and then dodge citations and condemnation were over. We didn't have to dodge those bricks anymore because Harold was in and it was a new day.

Harold Washington created a whole new era, and I don't think we will even turn back the clock. The Bible says "once you know the truth, and the truth shall set you free and you shall be free indeed." This means that once you learn how to ride a bicycle; once you've tasted a steak, you will never "unlearn" how to taste a steak. You may not have steak everyday, but at least you will have tasted a steak.

But the clock will not be turned back. There may be a slowing down. The fact that in the city two Black men are arguing about who is going to be the next mayor that has never happened in the City of Chicago before. And it means that we're not going to turn back the clock. We are going forward. Anytime you see While aldermen getting behind a Black man to be mayor, it means that the clock will not be turned back.

When we look at Black history, we will find that most changes in the black community came about through the Black church and the Black preacher. Not Turner was a Black preacher and he had a revolt during slavery time. All of our changes came through the black church, because that is the one social institution that we own. A Black preacher is free. In the Southern Baptist convention, a lot of my White brothers, wish they were as free in their pulpits and ministries as I am with this one. They are not free. That's the first thing. The second thing involved is that when we talk in terms of the Black church and politics, we find that politics have always been a part of religion. You can go back to your Biblical heroes in the Old Testament. Moses was a civil rights leader. God told him on the mountaintop, to go down and tell Pharaoh to let my people go." And if you took a profile of Moses and took a profile of King and a profile of Harold Washington, they would have more in common than not in common.

Jesus ministered to the total man. He fed them before he preached to them. On the mountain, the folks were hungry. He stopped a little boy and took his lunch, took a fish sandwich and made a supermarket out of it. So consequently, Jesus, before he preached to them, he fed them. The church must deal with the whole person.

I believe in a holistic ministry, a total ministry. I must feed a person, I must clothe a person. Once that person is clothed and fed, and has a home, now I can talk about salvation.

Harold Washington represented a symbol of hope for the Black Community. But not only a symbol of hope. Hope in the respect that he was the first Black mayor of this city, and not just the first black mayor, but the fact that he challenged the White power structure, and won. And he knew what he was doing. We were not putting a man in place because he was Black. He was not just a Black mayor; he was a mayor who happened to be black. He knew about finance; he knew about the economic structure; he knew the business structure; he knew the educational structure. He was a politician who knew how to politick.

Harold never forgot his roots. Harold knew that the people -- the guy on the corner -- put him in power; put him on the 5th floor. And he never forgot that. He would always go back to the people. Oftentimes, politicians (and I must say Black politicians also) forget from whence they came. Harold never forgot from whence he came. Now, as far as keeping his promises are concerned -- he kept his promises by keeping the Black community informed. We must understand the nature of politics -- it's compromise. And so consequently, a lot of things you'd like to do, you need time in which to do them, and unfortunately, Harold did not have enough time, He just did not have enough time. Had he stayed in another term, I believe without a shadow of a doubt that things would have been turned around, because he was just bringing the coalition of Whites into his realm of thinking. He certainly had it there before, but the fact is, he had to fight the philosophy that many Whites wonder about: "I kept you down all this time, now you're on top, you're going to push me down: and Black folk are not like that.

I think I would like to close with two points. The first is that it is my prayer that clergy persons, and especially Black clergy persons, embrace the philosophy and idea by the actions, not just words, that Jesus embraced. And that is to deal with the total man. Don't alienate politics from their ministry, because politics is not alienated from their ministry. We play politics in our churches. And so therefore, don't alienate politics. Go through the Bible and identify political appointees, Shadrack, Meshack and Adednego, Daniel (if you please). Identify civil rights leaders, Moses (if you please), and identify with those doing God's will. The second point I would like to conclude with is this. That it is my prayer that Black politicians will learn the philosophy, look at the life style (the political lifestyle, of course) of Harold Washington. See how he prepared himself, how he worked within the system until the system did not work with him, how he challenged that which was wrong, and how he triumphed over what was wrong, and the most important thing, that he kept his loyalty to the constituencies that elected him.

THE QUEST FOR UNITY AND IDENTITY IN THE EXPERIENCE OF HAROLD WASHINGTON

John Parker

Well, basically, I come out of the civil rights movement as an organizer with Martin Luther King, Jr. And, we've been trying to change the political machine in Chicago for a number of years. As a matter of fact in 1977, when Harold Washington first ran for mayor, I was then the president of the Westside Baptist Ministers Conference, and we supported Harold Washington because we felt that it was time for a change. And political hopes and aspirations for the black community were almost destroyed through the mayoralty of Jane Byrne. But then came the time, the right time; when the community selected Congressman Harold Washington to become a candidate for Mayor, and it seemed like a new day in Chicago.

As I was not then the president of the Conference because my term had expired, but thereafter I was the political coordinator, uh, it was tough because people were used to one kind of leadership. And that was the kind that the boss told the people primary obligation because I've always felt that those who have ability have the responsibility of making things happen, because we basically felt that there were only three kinds of people in the world: people who make things happen, people who let things happen, and people who don't know what's happening. So fortunately enough we were involved in the group that knew what was happening and we just went on to work and rolled up our sleeves and that was my basic role.

As political organizers, we always learned how to submerge our egos, because we knew that the movement, which let to the election of Harold Washington meant far more than self aggrandizement of any person or group. The people actually put that kind of trust into the movement. It was unlike any political campaign that I have ever experienced in the past, because it was spiritually by nature. Everywhere on the Westside of Chicago, we began to move into the churches. some preachers were reluctant to participate at first. They were waiting for someone else to take the initiative. Fortunately, I had a good friend, Rev. William Jenkins, who had worked with me for a number of years. He was one of the first pastors in the Westside Ministers Baptist Conference to allow Harold Washington to come to his church. When Harold Washington came to the church we had about 500 people there; and from this event the movement began to spread throughout the Westside area. No one was then reluctant anymore; they just opened up their hearts and became a part of the movement.

As political organizers, it was our responsibility to put together the kinds of political rallies that took place at the Pavilion Rally, where there were at least 20,000 people participating.

Harold Washington, in a real sense, represented a symbol of unity. Prior to his election, there were a number of clergy who had the westside/southside syndrome. The movement succeeded in breaking down this barrier. Clergy throughout the city came to the conclusion that there was no more westside, southside, or northside -- it was only one side to be concerned about and it was the Harold Washington side. And so we all got on that side and moved forward together.

Harold Washington galvanized the total community. He broke down the racial, ethnic, geographical, political and socioeconomic barriers which had traditionally polarized social groups. All persons began to fellowship and work together. The political process eventuated into an interdenominational movement. It consisted of Baptists, Methodists, Presbyterians, Lutherans, Pentecostals, and others. All religious denominations in the city came together to elect Harold Washington.

Now, what was it about Harold Washington that made this happen? Well, Harold has charisma. And it was really nobody like Harold Washington. First of all, he was the son of a preacher and he understood the black church. And Harold had the mannerisms of a preacher. He was known as a preaching layperson. He had a way with everybody. And that's what it was that kept people committed to the movement.

Harold had the common touch, and knew now to use it effectively. He related effectively with everybody: young, old, black, white, hispanic, asian; he just touched everybody. Previous mayors in Chicago were known as Mayor Daley, Mayor Bilandic, Mayor Byrne. But because he maintained the common touch, most people referred to Mayor Washington as Harold. He was extraordinary because people felt like he was a friend.

Many members of New Life Baptist Church worked with us in the movement. They were already oriented in the direction that to be a member of our church included also being a productive citizen. When you're 18 years old, you had to register to vote. So they knew that. If someone joined our church, we asked them some questions related to the Christian faith, asked them questions about the value of voting as it relates to being a citizen of this country, registered to vote.

And so, our church has always been politically oriented. The members were exuberant about participating in the Harold Washington political process and they were just ready, willing and able to go. As a matter of fact, in our church we also make a concentrated effort to know our political contest. We go through that in political education and everybody had to go out in their respective political wards and do some work for the Harold Washington campaign.

One of the things that our men did, because everybody was so enthusiastic about the fact that Harold Washington was a candidate, for the first time in any election that I can remember, all of the men took a block where they lived and went in the community knocking on doors. We kept some literature related to the campaign in church and people would come to our church looking for literature. We supplied them with the literature and they went out into the community disseminating it. And everywhere you looked, you say a blue button announcing the Washington campaign.

And I can remember that even when we went to the Pavilion that day, we had an afternoon church service. We shut down the church service and said we're going to reconvene church at the Pavilion. And all of our members came over. If you can remember it was a cold day. It was snowing, but the people decided that we had to go over and make it happen. Incidentally, that's the group that makes things happen. And a lot of people did this; there were a lot of people who said, well, church is out today; it's time to go over and support harold Washington. And that was really tremendous.

Well, originally it started out in the selection process. First of all, it was the first time in the history of Chicago politics that people selected the candidate rather than the party selecting the candidate. Because the people were involved in the selection process, they felt like Harold Washington was their candidate. Harold Washington was not forced upon the people. And so, the process started out like a campaign and ended up like a crusade. And that's one of the things that made the campaign a little different. That's how it all began in the churches; people prayed for Harold Washington, sang for him and they punched that punch for Harold Washington.

I think it was the first time in the history of Chicago politics that people felt so great about a candidate. And it was as though

Harold Washington was everybody's brother, cousin, or uncle. I have some members, who right now say, "Harold, that's my Uncle Harold." And some people would say "Do you know Harold Washington?" and they would say, "Yes, he's my uncle." Everybody wanted to be related to Harold Washington.

Another thing about Harold that was so unusual, is that he reached into the neighborhoods. That had never happened before in the black community. When Harold walked down the street, everybody would look up and see him coming and say "Hi, Harold!!!" Harold was quite personable.

Under his administration the streets of the city of Chicago were repaved. Sidewalks that had been torn up for years were reconstructed. The street sweeper started coming through the community more frequently. The garbage was being picked up; old cars were taken from the lots that had been there for years. Rehabilitation programs were taking place in the black community. It was almost like a new day and people were just engrossed in Harold Washington because he had the type of personality that galvanized the community and held them together.

That's important, because it is not enough to bring people together, you've got to hold them together. And Harold had that charisma. Things would not be like they are now in Chicago politics had Harold Washington lived longer.

However, I can say that the spirit of Harold is not really dead. He told us something before he left here to go and rest in heaven, that "I'm going to run this city from my grave." And our belief is that those of us who knew what Harold Washington stood for, would continue the spirit of the movement. And even today, I'm optimistic because I know the movement can overcome the political machine. And in this election that is coming up, part of our Harold Washington legacy is to put the political machine in the grave. We want to hold that political machine down and make sure it's dead. Because sometimes the political machine plays possum. And when we think the political is dead, it will pop up somewhere else. So we're just trying to put a nail in the coffin, and if we have to we're going to pour cement and concrete all around the coffin of the political machine because people in Chicago are unified.

But, I can remember an incident where Harold came up in church a little boy walked up to him, about 2 years old, and said "Momma, Harold Washington!" Harold picked him up, "Son, do you want to be the mayor!" And he said, "Well, I'm gonna stay in office and hold it until you get old enough to be the mayor!"

Harold Washington in his second term, I was called in to be his campaign coordinator in the 27th Ward. It was a tough race because there were a lot of candidates who had filed for alderman. And everybody wanted to hang on to Harold. and I was called in to sort out the stuff and get it back together so people wouldn't be dealing with their own egos. And we did that. And we turned out in the 7th Congressional District, about 70% and the Ward was second in the 7th which consists of several wards in terms of the vote. And I can remember Harold saying to me, "Well, you've been a long time supporter of me." And I said, "Yes, Mayor." He said, "Is there anything you want?" I said, "No, I think I'm gonna give you my autograph." And Harold said, "That will be a pleasure." That happened about one week prior to his sudden death.

*

We were going up to thank the mayor for the selection of Ricky Hendman and as we entered the elevators to go up, it was about 3 minutes after 11 on November 21st, and I saw a lot of the security people and being around him a lot, everybody knew me and I knew them, and I asked them a question, "What's going on? Is the mayor late?" Someone said, "The mayor's awful sick." And we were going upstairs and they were not letting anybody up and finally the paramedics were bringing him out and we felt then, our hearts were just suddenly beginning to bleed, because we looked at the mayor and he appeared to us to not be alive. And everybody in City Hall began to pray for Harold Washington.

And then later on when we really knew that he was not alive, we had decided that after talking to some elected officials and some committeemen that it was up to us to continue the legacy. And we've made up our mind to dedicate our lives, that we will have fairness in government, open, honest, and that we will make it what Harold Washington would have made it. And we're going to continue that process until that is achieved in the city of Chicago.

THE ROLE OF THE DISTRICT SUPERINTENDENT IN THE HAROLD WASHINGTON STORY

Charles Wesley Jordan

I was serving as a Superintendent in the UMC, Chicago Area, at the time when there were discussions around for a Black candidate for Mayor, and the possibility of Harold Washington servicing as that person. At a meeting that I had with the Black clergy of the Northern Illinois Annual Conference, it was suggested that we should have a meeting with Congressman Washington. The feeling was that my calling it as a Superintendent might, if you excuse the expression, give it some credibility. And we had remet shortly after Thanksgiving in the Fall of 1982. My understanding is that we were the first group of Black clergy in the city to meet with Harold Washington. We met in St. Mark United Methodist Church and we talked with him and then endorsed him. We said that we would be committed to a victory for him in the Primary. And that as pastors, we would have rallies in our churches and would attempt to mobilize our people. My commitment at that time was to be supportive of Harold Washington as a candidate. I first met him when he was a state representative. I was then in Rockford, Illinois serving as a Director of urban ministry for the UMC. He came to Rockford to participate in a panel discussion on the Kerner Report, the President's report on civil disorders. He was one of the panelists and I was extremely impressed with him and followed his career from that time on. I never realized, of course, that he would one day be the Mayor of the City of Chicago. Following then our endorsement, there were a number of rallies that took place in our churches. In January we had the first rally. In January of 1983, that rally was held at St. Mark, UMC. It was a rally consisting of Black United Methodists and other persons. We opened it up to other persons. I was asked to give greetings and some introductory remarks. It was important for participating clergy to know that I was supportive to them in my role as District Superintendent. In fact, Harold Washington himself asked some questions in this regard. I remember he asked Rev. Al Samson a question. He said, "I am a Methodist, and I know how Methodists operate." Then he asked, "are you out here doing this by yourself, are you guys getting out on a limb, or do you have the support of those who are in the hierarchy?" So. Rev. Samson said, "the hierarchy is here." So, indeed, all of us were impressed certainly as Harold Washington spoke to us and laid out before us his political platform and his vision for the city.

Well, I think, that the Cabinet, and the Bishop, Jesse DeWitt, at that time, were very supportive. Bishop Jesse Dewitt, expressed that support in some public ways. There was a prayer breakfast prior to the 1983 election, which was held at the Palmer House. Bishop Dewitt read the scripture lesson at that breakfast, and was the only major White judicatory person that was present on the platform at that time. Bishop Dewitt's involvement suggested that he was clearly in support of the Black United Methodist pastors as well as the District Superintendent.

An important thing to remember is that as a United Methodist Superintendent not only did I have responsibility to Black United Methodist pastors, but I also supervised churches that consisted of predominantly White congregations, some of them were White ethnic communities on the southwest side. So I felt that it was important that there be contacts made there. And at one of our District Pastors' meetings in 1983, in the height of the campaign, after the Primary, we had a pastors' meetings which was an interracial Black and White pastors'. At that time we drafted a letter for our conference paper about the concern for racism that was taking place in the campaign. While there was a message and a resolution that came from the District Pastors, when it appeared in the paper the only name that was there was mine because I was the Superintendent of the Chicago Southern District. I received a number of calls from some of my White pastors that were in ethnic communities expressing their concerns and fears they had in relationship to some of the expressions that were being made in their congregations. You know, there were many fears about the possibility of a Black Mayor, and what that was going to mean for the city. One fear was that the city was going to fall apart and utterly be destroyed. But there again, the pastors were sensing the need for my support. I have to admit, my pastors were on the front line. They were the ones that were knocking on doors and doing the precinct work, going to the meetings and so forth. I need to say that my role was not that of a campaign worker.

When the election was over, I wrote a letter to all of the Black clergy; it was a kind of victory letter, a letter of celebration. In that letter, I named those pasters that had been most involved in the campaign·and gave them special recognition.

I am aware that each one of use is an individual and certainly can operate out of that understanding of our own individuality as it relates to the political process or other things. I'm also aware that the work of a Superintendent, in being a supervisor of pastors, a pastor to pasters, a personnel administrator and a number of others things, it is extremely difficult. I would have liked to have been out there on the street during all the campaign. But I was also aware of the role and functioning of the Superintendent. It comes from that which is rooted in the word, sacrament and order. The Superintendent's function comes from the Bishop and the Superintendent relates to the local parish. The support of the local pastors is a function that, if taken seriously, includes sensitivity to the political and social needs of the community.

I think, in the long run though, the role of being a part of the judicatory leadership is a vital one, and is very necessary; and I found that the United Methodist pastors, my colleagues in ministry, who were in the local pulpits, felt much more secure in their efforts when they knew that they had the support of the judicatory.

There are five basic functions of the Superintendent, in terms of the specific tasks. The first one is supervision, which involves working with pastors and the Pastor Parish Relation committee, etc. Another is in the area of personnel, which has to do with the interpretation of the meaning of ministry, and working with pastors. Then there is the pastoral concern. The other two include administration and programs, which have to do with the District itself. As one things about these functions one becomes aware of how important they are to the life of the whole church. One can literally see that someone called the District Superintendent is a middle management person, a key link. Some would say it's the hardest job in the church. I don't know whether that's true or not, I would say it's different.

In January of 1987, we had a big rally at St. Mark Church, and the committee asked me to introduce the Mayor. I guess there were two feelings, one feeling of course was, well it certainly is an honor for me to introduce the Mayor. But when I realized the fact that there were so many persons in attendance who were front line people, pastors that had worked more closely with the Mayor, I knew that there asking me was an expression of appreciation for the role that I played as a District Superintendent. Because if you would have said, well, let's introduce the person who is closest to Harold Washington, that would not have included me. The one who has put in the most hours, that would not have included me. Therefore, I think it was a corporate thing. I was symbolic, as well as a representative of the community; but it was not a shallow representation, it was a genuine real representation. To a great degree I was a corporate representative. And I performed dual roles. The role of an individual and also a representative of the Black United Methodist religious community on the southside.

In presenting the Mayor I said, "It is a privilege to stand in this place and introduce the person for which this gathering is all about. Sisters and brothers our gathering is the celebration of the gifts, skills and experience of a proven leader. It is also a serious time as we commit ourselves to leadership by and for the people of this city. The question is no longer whether change and reform is possible in Chicago? The question is whether it will be allowed to continue? The question is not who can lead us in this endeavor, but rather who has already led us? Who is and will be the best Mayor for all the people? Who has, and will continue to provide equitable neighborhood development? Who has, and will continue to provide and implement affirmative action, confront racism, sexism and economic injustice. Who is it whose integrity has never been effectively challenged because it's authentic? Who is it who is strong and resilious and perseveres with a toughness that is not only capable of enduring to the end, but is encased in the mold of a Statesman? Who is it that sets religious value as an integral part of his political actions?" I then asked the people to stand and receive the Honorable Harold Washington, the Mayor of the City of Chicago.

THE SPIRITUAL LEGACY OF HAROLD WASHINGTON

Wilfred Reid

Harold Washington and I grew up together. We attended the same high school, DuSable High School. Our paths crossed each other constantly through high school. Our fathers were both ministers in the African Methodist Episcopal Church. We had a friendship in those days that was very tight and close because of our athletic abilities, and I think we both were quite surprised to discover years later that we would be in the mainstream of the political scene and religious affairs of the City of Chicago. Although we lost contact with each other after high school, we met up again a few years later. He was then a lawyer and congressman and I was pastoring St. Stevens AME Church, on the west side of Chicago. I remember a group of people in our church predicted back in the latter part of the 60s, and early 70s, that some day Harold Washington would be Mayor of Chicago. We had no idea that it would come to be true - it was a prophecy that came to light. I was pleased to be a part of the group that gave him full support, because I had a lot of confidence in this ability and felt that he could really make a real impact upon the City of Chicago. We lived to see the day when he made a significant impact not only on Chicago, but upon the State of Illinois and the country, as a whole. He gave to this city a sense of price. And to those persons who felt left out of the socioeconomic process, he gave them a new hope and the desire to feel that they were now becoming a part of the total life of the City of Chicago.

First of all, Harold Washington was charismatic. He was able to relate to people. A lot of people knew him as a congressman, a very successful congressman. They knew him as a good state representative. He was good at fixing and working with labor. He worked with the common people. He never pushed himself, but he was always in a position to do something for somebody else. And when the opportunity came for us to realize that he had a good chance to made a good run for Mayor of Chicago, I think he just had all the ingredients that it took to solidify that kind of relationship and base to draw all of us together. People just rallied around him because of his personality -- his dynamics, his ability to speak and his sense of making people feel that if you help me -- we can do it. He said, "we're going to move, this is it, let's go ahead."

Harold Washington served as a basis for identity within the Black church. He was a part of the Black church. He attended church and had a pastor. He went to his Pastor for counsel and consultation. I think people saw something valuable about that. He did not feel that he was above the worship experience. This served as a very helpful thing to a lot of people and especially to clergy that served as leaders in the movement.

The political success led by Harold Washington is consistent with the legacy of the African Methodist Episcopal Church. The African Methodist Episcopal Church was two hundred years old last year, eleven years younger than this country. And out of the African Methodist Episcopal Church came the feeling by Richard Allen of self improvement, moving forward and making things for ourselves. As a result of his philosophy and teachings, the first Black newspaper came out of the AME church. The AME Church also gave birth to black hospitals, the first banks, and schools of higher education. He gave us this feeling that we were somebody, almost two hundred years ago. The African Methodist Episcopal Church was a strong dynamic church and it's still a strong dynamic church that continues to play an influential part of bringing the black community together. All of this was due to the kind of philosophy and legacy that Richard Allen left for Black people back in 1872. Harold Washington comes along in the 1980s, and certainly left us another philosophy of moving forward. He gave to us the same kind of legacy as that developed by Richard Allen.

After Richard Allen, I think somewhere along the way, I think we got complacent. Many people did not know too much about Richard Allen. We forgot many years past. Martin Luther King, Jr. came on the scene and had to brush us up again, and give a sense of pride and a sense of direction. He died and then we went to sleep again. I believe Harold Washington came, again at the right time, to awaken us and to make us remember both the life of Richard Allen and Martin Luther King, Jr. Harold Washington lived in our day and hopefully some of us will be able to carry on this legacy so that young people can maintain a sense of pride. I just concerned and afraid that we soon forget, and in forgetting we become lazy and lose what we've gained. But I feel that Harold Washington came at the right time and made people wake up and review what needed to be done. This enabled us to come alive again and start moving forward, becoming a strong people.

I think Harold Washington's campaign complemented what I was doing because I've been militant all my ministry. A lot of times when you're singly doing something you look like you're by yourself, and people don't see what you are doing, they can't see the wisdom of it, or if there is no need to see the wisdom of it, they just sort of lay it aside and put you in a category and label you. But when he came along as a strong charismatic leader in the political arena and saying some of the same things, it only helped me to preach even harder, work harder to do the kinds of things I was trying to do to awaken the community. For instance, on the west side of Chicago, I organized the whole central west housing committee and wrote my masters thesis oat Northwestern, Garrett Theological Seminary on the "Black Church, The Impact of the Black Church Upon the Neighborhood," and out of that we were able to get housing. Malcolm X College was taken from Crain College and renamed in my office. Crain High School was renovated to the tune of over $800,000. We were able to bring

Black folk on the west side into the political scene. The Ed Davises, Danny Davises, and many others. People then could see that what we were talking about was a reality because, I think sometimes, we don't believe that a thing can happen and then we don't do anything to work with it. But Harold only helped to solidify, to complement, to give impetus to the fight that we were talking about. So, I think my preaching became prophetic, it became scriptural, it did all of the things that it needed to do to awaken people. And people started listening and I think we raised up many new young people, many new young adults and new families listening to the gospel and the church took on new life because of his outside leadership.

HAROLD WASHINGTON AND MARTIN LUTHER KING, JR.

NEW FRONTIERS IN CHURCH AND COMMUNITY

Darrell and A. P. Jackson

When I graduated from DuSable High School, Harold Washington was a freshman. I finished in 1937, he finished in 1941. But I knew of his father's law office on 47th and South Park; and I am aware of the area that he grew up in; we grew up in similar environments. I became acquainted with him when he emerged in the political arena, but I did not know him as a young man. Neither did I know him as a student at Roosevelt University and then a law student at Northwestern University. I knew him as he emerged in Springfield, Illinois, and later in Washington, D.C., and then back to Chicago. So I knew him in the latter part of his political career.

Well, when he went down to Springfield, quit naturally, we became acquainted with all the Black legislators down there because every now and then we would need a favor or two when election time came, so they always came by Liberty and we were very supportive of all our Black legislators in Springfield because they were down there fighting for our rights, Senator Newhouse and the rest of the fellows -- and Harold Washington was in that crowd. Of course, I felt a little closer to Harold because he was a "DuSable boy" and this sort of made our kinship a little closer. And, of course, when he was running for any office, Liberty would always go on record endorsing him, because I was a "DuSable boy." We were local boys who made good, I guess (if we made good).

As a legislator in Springfield, Harold Washington always stood out. Of course, there were persons in there that had seniority over him but he caught on real well as a freshman. And I think he was not satisfied with just being in Springfield. I think during the time he was in Springfield, he had his mind set on coming back to Chicago and running for an office in Washington. He captured that office, too, by the way. He did an excellent job while he was there.

I think his record in Springfield and his record in Washington were part of the number of factors that brought him to the forefront. We had too many politicians that were afraid of City Hall. There were too many preachers who were afraid of City Hall. There were not too many churches that welcomed any anti-Daley person. Harold Washington was never known as a Daley person. So, we found a kinship there. Both of us were independent of City Hall. Therefore, Harold Washington felt at home at Liberty Baptist Church (he was a Liberty many times before he became the Mayor of Chicago). In fact, he grew up on 47th Street, just two blocks away from Liberty Baptist.

My first involvement with Mayor Washington took place when he was Congressman Washington. During my last year at Garrett Evangelical Theological Seminary, I was appointed to the First Congressional Housing Task Force, thanks to my father and Liberty Baptist Church. So I came to know Congressman Washington at that time. I was elated just to be asked to be among so many other religious and civic leaders. He was not always at every meeting, but he always left an agenda of what he wanted us to do. I served on that committee for two years.

I first heard about Harold Washington as a State Representative. I knew he had tried to get Legislation through to make Dr. Martin Luther King's birthday a state holiday. That's when I first knew that he was really about some serious business. I knew he had thrown his hat in the ring with about five or six other Blacks in 1977, to run for mayor after Daley died, but, of course, we weren't politically well structured then, at least in the Black community,a t that time. But then when he decided to run for mayor with the help of the community, because I felt that he was the "people's candidate," he was the obvious choice. The first thing that came to my mind that I remember when working on Maynard Jackson's campaign to become Mayor of Atlanta when I was a student at Morehouse in 1973, is telling the brothers and sisters there that this will never happen in Chicago as long as I live (to have a Black mayor).

But my first real intimate contact with the mayor (and I'll never forget this), was on the third Sunday in January of 1983. There was a teachers rally for Washington at the church, just before the campaign in his first election. Whenever he would come to Liberty for political rallies, he would always come through the side door (49th Street door). Dad would be involved with something else and I would always meet him there with a couple of other officers and we would come up through the side steps (back steps) to my father's office. I remember he and I were walking up the steps and I said, "Congressman Washington, I want to ask you a question. I want to know if my alderman is with you in the campaign. A lot of the aldermen have not come out and said whether they were going to support you or not, and I want to know if my alderman is with you. My alderman, at that time, and still is in the sixth ward, Gene Sawyer. He said, "Jackson, he's with me, but he can't announce it just yet. He will be announcing it soon." This is the thing that he told me that I never will forget as long as I live. I still had a few doubts about whether he could make it. He said, "When people believe in this campaign, we're going to win," but you've got to believe. And I told him as we went into my father's office, "You have converted me on these steps" and from that point on, I preached Mayor Washington, Mayor Washington, Mayor Washington -- we can do it, we can do it, we can do it. I even converted my grandmother, who was a diehard Daley person. So that was my first real encounter with Harold.

I went to school, of course, in Atlanta. I used to preach at Ebenezer Baptist church on Sunday evening when there were about 40 people present. The Pastor, Martin Luther King, Sr., would allow the students to practice on his congregation. Of course, Martin Luther King, Jr. was nine years younger than I was and while he was outside shooting marbles or doing something else, we were inside learning how to preach. I was a student at the School of Religion at Morehouse. I didn't become acquainted with Martin Luther King, Jr. until 1956, in Detroit, Michigan, at the Cadillac Hotel. That's when I got to know Martin real well. Martin remembered his father talking about my father and so we were preachers' kids together. At that time Martin had not risen to the heights that he eventually came to realize when he began to start his protest movements and then he came to Chicago and let us know that we were still on the plantation, even in Chicago. He said Chicago was an extension of Mississippi, which is true, and we thought we had it made here. He came and let us know that we were still segregated and discriminated against. He went into the economic phases of the civil rights movement and he would come every Friday to Liberty (this was when we had Operation Breadbasket). We would plan our strategy as to how to boycott the Coca Cola Company and bread companies. Believe it or not, at that time blacks did not drive bread in Chicago or soft drink trucks. They were helpless and we thought we had it made in Chicago. I remember Dr. King said he wanted the leader of Operation Breadbasket not to be a preacher, not to be a pastor, because he knew pastors and the jealousy of the pastors. So, Jesse was around and Jesse was in school out to Chicago Theological Seminary and Jesse became the leader of Operation Breadbasket. We would meet every Friday at Liberty to plan our strategy and Dr. King would give us our instructions for the week. That gradually evolved into the political structure of meeting on Friday. Whenever there was a rally to be held, there was no other place to go to but Liberty, because Dr. King was at home there, and the people associated him with Liberty. Also Liberty was a free church. This was important to Dr. King because he could say anything he wanted to and my hands were not tied by City Hall, like a lot of the other clergy (through no fault of their own). Dr. King was always welcome. Not only did he have his political rallies at Liberty, but he preached many times at Liberty. I used to pick him up by myself at O'Hare and bring him to the church. He would always talk about what a pleasure it was to be at Liberty, at another preacher's son's church. So quite naturally, when the rallies and marches came about, the pivotal point was meeting at Liberty on Sunday afternoon to go into Cicero and so forth.

Martin and Harold Washington were two of a kind. Harold Washington was concerned about folks. You see, I've never known a mayor who could be called by his first name. Folks in Harlem saw Mayor Washington and would say, "Hi, Harold." He was the peoples' mayor. Martin was just as down to earth as he could be in spite of his Nobel Peace Prize and all of that. He was still Martin to all the guys who knew him. I think Harold and Martin were about the same thing -- better housing, better job,s equal rights for women and so forth. They were about the same thing in both of their political and economic philosophies.

Well, I think you can even go back to my grandfather, who pastored Liberty from 1925 to 1950, who was quite liberal in his outlook in those days. The few Black politicians we had during that time came to Liberty. They had an association with the pastor, with the church and its membership. This, of course, filtered through to my father and Liberty stands for its name. It really means liberty. My father stated that people could feel free in the church. The philosophy has been this way and we've always had a philosophy at Liberty that God is first, we believe in the teaching of the Bible. We believe in having members Biblically literate. We also want them to be socially sensitive. Over the years we have educated our members not only to the word of God, but we also educate them to the world. So Liberty has always been open to politicians and different leaders coming into the church to speak.

I remember the days too when Dr. King came. I was young at the time and I do remember going with my father a few times to the airport to pick up Dr. King. I was just, you might say, in awe of him. I would always listen to him and my dad talk. Dr. King was always very down to earth. I knew that Dr. King was fighting for human rights, trying to make the world better. Because I was raised in Chicago, I did not know what my brothers and sisters were going through in the south, except for what I saw in TV; But, I knew something significant was happening. I saw people fighting for voter registration, while watching water hoses and dogs being turned on them. I knew something needed to be changed. I came to the realization a little bit later that in the north the same racial hatred was here, but it was hid behind a grin and a pat on the back. So when I looked at Dr. King, I knew what he stood for. I began to become aware of the importance of equal rights, and social awareness. When Dr. King died, I was a freshman in high school, so I was well aware of what was going on. As a matter of fact, he died on that Thursday, April 8 and that Tuesday, April 2 we had just had a walk-out of Hirsch High School so that we could have Black History taught in the Chicago Public School system. There had been a series of walkouts that Tuesday.

When I compare Dr. King and Mayor Washington, I think of it this way, Dr. King has a vision and he instilled it in us, through his many speeches, and demonstration of nonviolence. Mayor Washington became a reality of that dream, and for people of my generation, I would say anyone in Chicago was really charged up with Mayor Washington. Because we had heard that this could possibly happen. But it was becoming a reality and is always exciting to be a part of living history. I tell the young people at church all the time, you're a part of living history. We had the first Black astronaut, the first Black Miss America and then with Mayor Washington. I tell them all, you're living with living history, you're a part of it. To me, the exciting thing was just to be a part of this history making movement in the City of Chicago, and to know that I played a small part.

Both of them realized that power was with the people. Regardless of what people might say and do, both Dr. King and Harold

Washington felt that the church is a power base that we cannot afford to ignore; so they were with the people all the time.

I confronted Harold Washington once or twice for not coming back to Liberty to say thank you; when he finally got around to doing it, I realized that everybody was looking for him. But he came to Liberty many times. In fact, we were together for Dorothy Tillman voting day in October and I confronted him again because he hadn't been back to Liberty. He said, "let me tell you something, Pastor Jackson, you're my second pastor. If I go to your church too often, my first pastor will get mad at me." He would always so to me "here's my second pastor."

I didn't have to come out and say, "I'm for Harold Washington." The people knew this. In fact, the members of Liberty have always taken pride in the fact that Liberty is an independent church and the officers of Liberty make sure that the pastors do not want for anything. So my hands are free and the members feel the same way about it. So we do not have to come out every time something happens with, "what is your position on this?" My position is always on the side of social justice and human rights. So we don't have to come out and keep repeating our answers on emerging issues.

I think first of all it is really an honor to be able to work along with you father. I think this is the thing that both Martin Luther King, Jr. and Mayor Washington had an opportunity to do, to work with their fathers. I've learned that it's always good when working with your father to keep you eyes and ears open and your mouth closed sometimes, and really observe. Take criticism the correct way, don't get mad. Sometimes things may be a little slow and you want them to be a little faster, but you have to learn to be kind and patient. Many times things open up.

As I look at leadership in relationship to Mayor Washington, he was more than just a folk hero. People say "folk hero" and to me when you say folk hero you think of someone who is almost a myth, even though it does take on something else. But Mayor Washington was more than just a folk hero. He was an example of what can e done. Not only did he open our eyes politically, but he opened our eyes to say you can do it. If people believe in you enough, you can do it. And for me, he has inspired me, not only from knowing him on a personal basis, but to know how he impacted Chicago, the United States, and the world; he helped us to know that if you believe in something strong enough, you can make it happen. Recently, I preached a sermon on "Touch the World" and the main point I was trying to get across in this sermon was if we all work in our own little parts of the world, we can make a change. We can't just change the world on an individual level. And I think Mayor Washington serves as an example of what it means to make a change. Look what he did just in Chicago and how he really sparked the political interest in people all across this country. Jesse Jackson is doing a similar thing.

I really thing Harold Washington was a challenge to Black manhood. I am discouraged to a certain extent and dismayed when I see Black women being pushed into positions like anchor women on TV, when Harry Porterfield is pushed aside. I think the White man is trying to say to the Black man, "You are nothing" and to the Black women, "Your man is nothing." I'm dismayed because a lot of us are buying that and a lot of Black men have lost their inspiration and aspiration. It's the system. We have very few Black men succeeding today. Some might say that Harold Washington had it made from the go-get, because of his father. Harold was a runner for his father when he was a precinct captain. They tell me that I've got it made because of my father. they forget that folks are folks, and the more you have, the more trouble you've got to contend with. But the thing that bothers me most is that I don't think Black males have accepted this challenge.

I think that's why we have to do down to DuSable and other high schools as ministers and talk to our Black children. I met a girl who was going to Spellman College in Atlanta, Georgia, and she was miserable because she had a low grade in math. We tell our teenagers that they are a part of the church. I talked to my daughter-in-law who teaches at Spellman and she says that Spellman is going to raise the level of admittance to 3.5 next year. These kids went down there with a "C" average and got in, but not now. It's going to be like that all over.

Well, I just thank God that I have been privileged to walk with me like Martin Luther King and Harold Washington. I thank God that we walked together, that we saw things eye-to-eye. We had the same feelings about issues that confront life and I feel that as I said one Sunday at church, that Dr. King was never talking about going to heaven, he wanted to live down here. And I'm not going to preach about heaven and dying. Dr. King believed in life. Jesus believed in life. So I just thank God that I was encouraged to hold my position on the preaching of the Gospel to make it relevant, to make to live and to also try to be a living example of the Gospel myself.

As my father was talking, I was reminded of something as we were looking at a coalition between Mayor Washington and Dr. King, and I think one of the greatest moments I can remember of being in the presence of Mayor Washington was in January 1985, as the city celebrated the birthday of Martin Luther King, Jr. My father was invited to speak at Madonna Temple that evening of the celebration. He and Rev. Arthur Brasier were the only two ministers that spoke and my father was on the program early along with Ester Rolle from Good Times. There were a lot of other stars there. Dexter King spoke. Oprah Winfrey was there. I got a chance to go backstage and Stevie Wonder was going on later, but we couldn't stay because it was kind of late. But for my father to be there on this program meant a lot to me. I never will forget it. I was sitting in the balcony. After Dad spoke I met him downstairs, and Mayor Washington was talking with him. He said, "here's young Jackson." So we were standing there with Mayor Washington in a section with some dignitaries and Mayor Washington introduced us to Alderman Pucinski. Mayor Washington started introducing us to other people and here I was, celebrating Martin Luther King's birthday with the first Black Mayor of Chicago, being introduced along with my Dad to a host of other accomplished persons. This was a great moment for me. I guess that's the way to kind of sum it up. Moses had a vision. Moses lead the people. He led them through the wilderness experience. He taught them things. He let them know what they could expect. All he saw was the promised land, but he never went. I think Dr. King had a vision. He began to see that vision take shape. He had his glimpse of the promised land. He even said he would never get a chance to get there. Mayor Washington had a vision of a promised land for Chicago. He laid down the track. He laid down the foundation. He opened our eyes. And we must keep our eyes on the prize, as they say. Can't close them now, they're too far open. Too many people have opened up our eyes and we just can't fall back.

NEW DIRECTIONS AND COMMUNITY AND CHURCH DEVELOPMENT

THE LEGACY OF HAROLD WASHINGTON

Myron McCoy

As I think about Harold Washington, my first meeting with him was after his election as congressman in the first congressional district. I was often working with Macio Pembroke who served on his housing task force. Harold Washington had a first congressional housing task force.

Macio Pembroke was the senior minister, at that time, of Saint Mark United Methodist Church. Interestingly enough, in 1977, when blacks attempted to support Harold Washington for mayor, Macio was on the blue ribbon committee. Then he helped in the campaign of the first congressional office. He also served on that task force. He also served as an adjunct Professor at Garrett Evangelical Theological Seminary, Evanston, Illinois. I've had the benefit not only of working with Macio at St. Mark United Methodist church, but also of being a part of his class at Garrett. Then, my next encounter with the congressman was at Macio's funeral. He came back to give a testimonial of their relationship.

Following that, late in 1982, there was discussion again of a need for a black person to run after many things precipitated by Jane Byrne in which she took some blacks off the school board and added segregationist whites. These things represented a slap in the face of the black community. There was a strong feeling that we needed a black person for Mayor. Harold Washington stood out as a congressional man with stature. also he had made the attempt to run in 1977. So, I felt committed to him as part of that legacy of knowing some of his prior commitments to the community and also to the church. I had a deep respect for Macio Pembroke and Harold Washington. I believe that their spirits were genuine.

My first encounter, as part of the campaign, was early on circulating petitions within church trying to get Harold Washington on the Democratic primary. The Harold Washington phenomenon did not catch on with the black church instantaneously. I can remember seeing people dodge the person with petitions for fear of having their name identified with it. The black community had that much fear from the white political forces in the city.

After that, United Methodist clergy came together and sponsored the first church rally for Harold Washington at St. Mark United Methodist Church. I became more involved in the campaign in a different kind of way. After the rally, the media had a kind of conspiracy against the Harold Washington campaign ever getting off the ground. I think they did the newscast of that first rally. They focused their cameras on an empty pew, suggesting that this black, middle-class church, was really not in support of Harold Washington. We had the rally on a Friday night. That Sunday morning, I preached a sermon in which I asked the members of the congregation to call that television station and state the fact that we wanted fair representation from the media regarding campaign appearances of Harold Washington. We thought it was poor taste of theirs to overlook an entire congregation and focus on an empty pew, suggesting that folks were not really enthusiastic about this kind of campaign. Oddly enough, I do not know whatever happened to the women but I do know that she did not continue as a newscaster; she was no longer affiliated with the station at the end of the campaign. It got people started monitoring how the news media was portraying the campaign. I think it was a groundswell of a movement taking place throughout the city.

Harry Gibson and I did not want to get St. Mark United Methodist Church directly involved with the campaign. Therefore, we organized a particular group of persons that were interested in the Harold Washington campaign. We gave them encouragement to move forward, as they sponsored rallies, became the deputy registrars to register people to vote, and did some knocking on doors. Then, leading up that first primary, I can remember the church being a busy hive, as folks took off from work and prepared sandwiches to send to all the different poll watchers.

It was a tremendous kind of experience that I'd never seen before. As it merged together, middle-class blacks united with those who were not middle-class. It was the only time that I have seen this happen at St. Mark UMC. Churches attract a certain kind of people and during the campaign those kinds of people who were not normally attracted to the church came to the church to be a part of the movement when rallies were held.

The church also served as a kind of headquarters. We encouraged people to have the different group meetings in the fellowship hall of the church. Members of this church had not been allowed to participate in a meaningful way as a congregation in the Harold Washington movement in 1983, so for 1987, early on, we did the same kind of thing in allowing the formulation of a group of persons who were interested, we always made it known that folks who had other candidates could organize groups. But none did. Our group got busy with voter registration.

They were the Willing Workers. The nonofficial appendage of the church. They all went and had training as deputy registrars and sat in supermarkets and stood on corners registering people. In fact, they registered close to 800 or more different persons for the last campaign. They also sponsored a couple of rallies within the south shore community in which Martin Luther King III was one of the guests. We were trying to get members to see that they do participate in the political process and that the church should be involved in helping to create a little bit of God's kingdom here on earth.

Now, let me say a word about the time test of effective leadership. What I could suggest is that it's important, as the church grows and get involved in programs and ministries, that the life of those programs and ministries should live beyond the pastor, or any charismatic leader. The only way that happened is by people having some direct ownership in the process. And then, for me, if it continues after the leader is gone, that says the work was effective. I think the true testimony of Harold Washington's leadership is that the interest of the community is still high, people want to be a part of the political process and they want to share ideas of how government should be operated. And although blacks, at this point, are dickering between two potential candidates for Mayor, where before we never even had the reason to think that we would have the opportunity to share in the process.

We need to structure ourselves in the kind of way in which folks do not have to hesitate in participating in leadership. Leadership consists of persons who have been around for over 20 years as well as persons who have not been around very long. What we're suggesting is that it is always time to serve and to participate in the leadership of an organization. We need to create the kind of environment in which persons can see and experience God's call in their life. Whether it is to enter the ordained ministry or to look at a secular job, it's important to realize that we all have a part to play. There are no big shots, nor little shots, but it's everyone doing their part that makes the ministry of the entire congregation meaningful.

Take collaborative leadership, working together as a team has to be the way to go in the future. They helped by allowing me to participate with them in decision making. I helped them work through problems and shared some of their hopes and dreams, and frustrations. All have come to benefit me. I had a kind of storage case back somewhere that I could refer to and pull on when the time arose for me to step in and make a decision. And I must say that in those situations, history will suggest that when I had to step in for the two of them, we never lost a beat. And that's the way it should be.

TOWARD A MINISTRY OF CARING

HAROLD WASHINGTON AND THE FUTURE OF THE BLACK CHURCH

Nathaniel Jarrett

I appreciated Harold Washington's quality of service as a congressman and as a state senator. I felt that he was a black man imminently qualified to give leadership not only to the black community, but to all levels of government for all people. And then when the decision was made by Congressman Washington to run for the office of mayor, there seemed to have been a moment a *kyrios* moment that became a tide that just caught people up in it, whether they wanted to get caught up in it or not, it just carried them away. And I got caught up in it emotionally, psychologically and spiritually. I invested time, and became excited; and our church became involved. And that's basically the genesis of my involvement.

In particular, our denomination -- the African Methodist Episcopal Zion church -- has been involved historically, when there was a fight for justice and equality. Whenever the issue is one of freedom, the AMEZ is always involved. Frederick Douglass was a local preacher in the AMEZ church. Sojourner Truth and Harriett Tubman were members of the AMEZ church. The Right Reverend Stephen Gill Spottswood, who was the chairman of the board of the NAACP for about twenty years -- served as a bishop in the AMEZ church. So that our history clearly mandates involvement. The Harold Washington situation was for me personally, a social justice issue. And the prophet Micah tells us that one of the things that God requires of us, is to do justly, or to do those things which bring about liberation and reconciliation in relationships.

So, involvement in the political process was consistent with our understanding of the nature and purpose of the church. Clearly it was an imperative to be involved, not just in the political process, but in addressing the issue of social justice. If it were only a matter of politics, I would not have been involved; but there were ethical and moral issues involved. There were issues of right and wrong.

I viewed Harold Washington as an instrument to address questions of social justice. I believe that he, too, became caught up in something that was much bigger than himself. Also, the moment was right. The movement started and the moment swept up Harold Washington and carried him to heights that were perhaps even surprising to him. I think the movement was greater than Harold Washington as a person. And certainly we felt that he was the person who could give the kind of moral leadership that could speak to the kinds of justice issues that we felt needed to be addressed. We felt that it was a time of redemption in a real sense for the political system in the city of Chicago. But I would clearly want to reemphasize that it was bigger than any one man.

If it were not Harold Washington representing the movement to redeem the community and serve the community, then the God of social justice would have had someone else to do the job. Thank God it was a person as capable as Harold Washington. It was more than the man. The issue of social justice was much more than the man and the movement focused on the issues that were essential to quality of life and the redemption of community. It dealt with a just government and the provision of human services for all of people.

I would certainly say that the clergy groups that were involved in the process clearly understood a part of their role to be prophetic. And accountability automatically goes along with that prophetic role. A lot of us made it clear to Harold Washington and to others that we were not in it for self gain; we were not wanting anything for ourselves or for our churches, but we were in it because of social justice issues. And while we were supporting him in that situation, if he ever violated that trust, if he ever went contrary to the good of the people, we would do the appropriate thing. We would become as active in removing him from office as we were in placing him in office. Therefore, a accountability was crucial and critical.

We were not looking to replace one system of oppression and one system of patronage that was white one that was black. That was not our concern; but rather we were concerned with making politicians that were elected to be servants of the people.

There was a coalition that transcended racial and ethnic barriers. It was not as broad as many of us desired relative to white involvement, but it was a pioneering effort. It was the beginning. It certainly reflected a coalition between black and hispanics and some of the white community. Clearly it demonstrated that those with power were not going to willingly surrender power, and it was the whites who had the power. And as a result of that, the broader-based white communities did not support Harold Washington. It was not because he did not attempt to reach out to them, but they had much invested in the old system, in the old way. And they were not looking for another day. They were not looking to be led by a black man.

Harold Washington understood the spirit of the oppressed. He manifested in a real sense, the life of the oppressed. And as a result of that, he, himself, was recognized as a champion of the oppressed, and he was perceived as such. The opposition did things that even more projected the image of Harold Washington a an oppressed person. The press, the white community, you name it, they were all forces that were working against him. It was easy for those themselves felt oppressed, to identify with him and to rejoice and celebrate the victory. It seemed that it was our victory. Not only black people, but all oppressed persons found joy, I think, in his victories.

Let me say it this way. Early on in my life, I realized that I was cared for. As a youngster growing up in Montgomery, Alabama. And then as an older child growing up in the ghettos of Detroit, Michigan, I sensed that somebody cared for me. As a teacher in the public schools of Detroit, Michigan and later as a seminarian at Yale Divinity School, doors opened that I didn't know were there. Things somehow always fell into place for me. So when I started by DMin program at Chicago Theological Seminary, I was asked to come up with a word that seemed to characterize my ministry. I was asked to reflect on my ministry and at that time I had been in the ministry for perhaps 15-20 years. As I reflected on it, the word "caring" emerged as most characteristic of my ministry. I clearly felt that I had been cared for. And it became for me an imperative to care for others.

So we have attempted to design a ministry of caring. Caring in the holistic sense.

I am convinced that Harold Washington's image and his style was imminently exemplary of the caring personality. You could not know him and not feel his genuine care at every level of government. He, indeed, was a carer. We were inspired and reminded that in the midst of hostility and aggression perpetrated on us by others, that we could still care. In the midst of his struggle, the caring quality was always present. That was a source of inspiration. As a politician early on, he cared for the people; he provided services for the people. It was fundamental to his understanding of who he was and what it meant to be a servant. Certainly we were inspired by that. And it became a sort of a model for us.

The people here at Martin Temple, on one occasion I asked them to share with me why there were so enamored with Mayor Washington, and what was it about him that so attracted them. And they invariable would say, he cares; he's not seeking a kingdom for himself and he's not lining his pockets. But he cares for blacks, women, hispanics, you name it. Anyone who took the time to objectively study the life of Harold Washington, it seems to me, had to conclude that he was a carer. And that certainly inspired us.

Now, let me just say a word about something that impressed me regarding the movement. There was a togetherness within the black community that I have never in my life experienced. Now that was because the moment was right, the message was right, and the man was right. There was a spirit that Harold Washington possessed which made you feel that you wanted to be a part. He was on the verge of introducing the kind of government and society that would indeed be characterized by social justice, brotherhood and sisterhood. There was an excitement that enabled us, perhaps for the first time to forget about the factors that divided us -- southside blacks, westside blacks, black Roman Catholics, black pentecostals, and black Methodists. Although the array of denominations, personalities and backgrounds were a joy to behold, for once in my life, I felt that we had become one people, sharing a common goal, a common vision, one perceiving a common destiny. That this is what God had created us to be.

SPIRITUAL FORMATION AND COMMUNITY DEVELOPMENT AS MANIFESTED IN HAROLD WASHINGTON

Hycel B. Taylor

Well, I can't claim the kind of personal relationship with Harold that certainly other ministers in Chicago have had. Because of my commitment to his pursuits to be the Mayor, I had him here at Second Baptist Church on two occasions during his first campaign. Thereafter, we were in contact with each other, in terms of serving in his campaign and raising funds for him. When I was the President of Operation PUSH, it was at that time that I encountered him more often. The first instance I had meetings on several occasions with him to talk about the City, the problems he was encountering with the City Council, his relationship to the Black aldermen, and how I could help with that.

On one occasion when I met with him, I was uncertain about certain things that he was doing and I had to challenge him. But he, in his style, was able to respond to my concern satisfactorily. But he was good at soothing you in that manner.

In the first instance, my admiration for Harold Washington motivated me to invite him to come to Second Baptist as guest speaker. We don't have a lot of leaders of his calibre and I certainly wanted this congregation to be informed; but I also knew that he needed the support of the people here in Evanston. He made clear that Evanston is just in the backyard of Chicago, which is truly the case, and when Chicago gets a cough, we catch a cold over here. So that was a part of it. But I've always brought major leaders to this church, so that our people could be in contact with them. And then, the constituency of Second Baptist church includes so many people who are from Chicago; so he had a chance to get a great deal of support from the church.

I think in all cases we have to measure realistically what a Black Mayor can bring to a city that is dominated by a White power structure, and all the racist implications of that. And certainly Harold did not have the base of power, nor the personal authority to effect a great deal of change on behalf of Black people. However, on a symbolic basis, he brought so much to us. Harold was a unique character and he had an extraordinary capacity to be everybody's person. He related across the board from the ghetto persons to the highest; and being a son of Chicago, that enhanced his presence all the more. So in a way, you have what I call vicarious achievement; by his achieving, all achieved. Notwithstanding, that left a lot to be desired because symbolic power is not actual power. In the last analysis, the benefits that accrued to Black people are minimal in terms of economics. But for the tenure that Harold was there, without question he gave Black people a new sense of hope, a future and possibilities that are not all being realized at the moment. A great portion of his magnitude was in modeling for Black communities self-esteem, identity and hope.

Unfortunately, that is so limited. One can't say that for the masses of Black people the quality of life changed dramatically because of Harold Washington's presence there. There's always an elite group, people who can benefit. And indeed, we have seen that. So, the benefit economically, and in terms of real power, is small. But he did change the character of Chicago politics tremendously and the reform is not so much when the patronage went out, but the reform was one that Black people now can see themselves as potential power brokers in the City. And if the future holds any possibility that we can maintain the spirit of Harold Washington, then we can not only achieve symbolic power, but through our collective action, we can achieve real power in the City; and I hope that will be the next phase of what we do.

Harold must be perceived in relation to the black church because Harold fits into the scheme of what leadership has always been for Black people. The Black church is obviously the real community organization in the community, Chicago especially. No real power exists apart from the Black church. It's the only organization in the Black community that has a power base to support itself, to which a leader like Harold Washington or Jesse Jackson or anyone else could go, without having to get permission from White people. So it was the base of power that was there for his campaign to become the Mayor.

But not only that, one has to think theologically about that as well, because there was with Harold at the outset, no clear sense that he was anything other than an ordinary politician. One reached out and grabbed Harold because he had a special charisma. That was added on by the church. I saw that at Operation PUSH when they brought him in. There was a kind of anointing with Harold which added a dimension of charisma to him, a kind of holiness, that was not there, in my judgment, until the church put its approval on him. And, of course, during the first years of his administration, the night before we campaigned, we literally laid hands on him at Operation PUSH. We did it as we would anoint any minister. It was a very holy moment, so there is a sense of transcendence that was a part of his work that added his effectiveness. When he died, we say not just the burial of a politician, but the addition to him of a holy man. I don't think Harold always knew that he was holy.

Now, did the black church adopt Harold, or did Harold see his political success to be possible only in regard to the potential within the Black church?

Well, it's a curious problem because most politicians, if they could get along without the Black church, I think they would. There were times when I felt that Harold came to the church only because it was a necessity for him and his power base. That's why I'm saying that he may not have always seen himself in that kind of religious or prophetic category that we had given to himself. The people had anointed him, you see, and I'm not sure he always saw himself in that light. I would not altogether suggest that he did not recognize the authority or the power of the church, but Harold was always aware of his need for radical autonomy, especially from preachers in Chicago. They exert so much power until Harold did not want the black church to dictate directions to him.

One of the critical points was always that Harold had to demonstrate he was the Mayor and not Rev. Jesse Jackson, so that tension was always there with the church. Harold in some sense, rose to the point in which he exercised almost complete ecclesiastical authority himself; because he would go to the churches and present himself along side the ministers. So, that kind of strength is the attribute of holiness that he gained because the ministers respected him and would allow him to do it.

So his autonomy was both in the sense that he transcended the authority of the clergy, but at the same time, he played the humble role with them that invited him in almost a patronage way. And that's a part of his unique character. He could be on both sides; he could be above you and below you at the same.

Now, let me attempt to give a theological analysis of the connection between the political career of Harold Washington and the Black church. It includes the element of transcendence, on the one hand, and then the concreteness of centering where the power was, on the other hand. Few other leaders would have had the power to cohere the community and bring it to a sense of oneness, so it could act with one will. The church alone had the authority to do that and that to me is a statement about its godliness. In his transcendence, Harold was a symbolic leader, which meant that there were no great material benefits that would accrue to the Black community. He represented transcendence, but the Black church alone could grant to him that transcendence, which created a kind of spiritual unity that had its authority and which White people feared. It was often asked of me when I was PUSH, "Is this campaign a crusade?" One would have thought it was similar to a revival. But what they were seeing was a dynamism, a phenomenon that transcended the structural dimension of the campaign. It had an element of mystery. White people could not understand. They asked what is this thing? We had a kind of pentecostal gathering, and many things happened under that condition. New relationships occurred and a new sense of who Black people were developed out of that. The church renewed itself in the sense of what its mission is. We found that the church itself is a political force to be reckoned with in the political arena, and we played with that to see how far we could go; we feared its potential.

When we are one with God, we become personally indivisible, spiritually with God. God centers us with a new sense of authority and power. At the same time, when we become one people, indivisible, then there is a power center that is far more tremendous and frightening. I think it becomes the operative principle of unity and oneness, to act with one will, and to act with one authority.

In the instance of Chicago, people were able to transcend the limitations of their physical slavery and to see that the exercise of spiritual unity has enormous power potential.

We did it by accident, and that's why I say Black people were shocked. When there were great gatherings at PUSH and other places and we went into almost a kind of pentecostal ecstasy, we couldn't contain it, we could not carry it to its logical extreme. What we have seen, was that after Harold was in office, then everybody was asking, "how do we maintain this kind of energy," because it quickly goes down.

What the experience of Harold Washington's campaign showed us, is the degree which we are not in control of our spiritual potential. We are not knowledgeable enough about it, nor do we have the capability of harnessing it. I always thing of the black church as a nuclear reactor. But it would be unfortunate for that reactor to be there and generate all that power and there are no power lines to carry it to something with certain functions. So our churches are like great spiritual reactors. On Sunday morning we generate all kinds of power, but there's nothing connected to it. I doesn't go anywhere. You don't see any large towers and wires as it were. Why is it that we can generate so much power to put a Black mayor in or to put a Black president almost in, with Jesse Jackson, and yet knowing that it only essentially a symbolic move and we can't benefit from it? The why is that slavery (400 years of it) so damaged our minds and creates so much doubt and faithlessness in us, that once we have an experience of power, our faith is not there to carry it through. I think that the Black church has preached the faith that allows for the formation of spirit, if we can use that term, but at the same time never though of that spirit manifesting itself in material or social rewards. It is ethereal, you know, it just mystifies, like steam; it just floats out into the air. Wherever there is spiritually, there is also a material product that ought to be the consequence of it. This seems to be consistent with the spirit of God. God creates stuff. How is it that we can be so spiritual, but not create anything. That's because of our mental slavery. We feel guilty about money. We feel guilty about power, even to the creation of power and exercise of power. I can even tell you that during Harold Washington's campaign, there was a moment when we exercised power and then felt a little bit guilty about it, because when power is exercised it also counters other power and subdues them.

If the mental shackles are broken and we become free to create as a consequence of that unlimited spiritual potential that is there, we would become full participants, uninhibited participants, in this society. Not merely just to accommodate it and to be what it is, but by virtue of our participation we would radically alter it. It would never be the same. If we had the faith to carry through our spirituality, in terms of economic development, the first principle is that we would become a unit of solidarity for economic development. Our resources would not be so fragmented. For example, the Black church itself, needless to say, economically is a wealthy organization. Every Sunday, we take up enough money at the 11:00 a.m. service to save Provident Hospital, Fisk University and Bishop College, which are dying. We have the resources and we do it. If we exercise the principle of unity that our faith gives to us, the oneness of God, the oneness of each other, and the principle of tithing, we would not have to have a welfare system by White people. Then if you move beyond that, entrepreneurs would become conglomerates, joint ventures could take place, we would become masters of economics and use our resources in a collective way rather than in an individualist way here and there. It seems to me that Harold Washington represents to us what Black aspiration is for all of us. The tragedy is that Harold Washington or Jesse Jackson are only individuals. Our reliance is too heavily upon the symbolic leaders. Vicarious achievements are never sufficient. Now what we have to do is translate what happened with Harold Washington and our participation in making that happen into the coming life of all of us, so that Harold Washington, Andy Young, Marion Berry or any others will not be looked up to as satisfying the requirements for the masses of the people. We must get to that place, and the church must see the possibility of the potential in doing this, where all of our people will benefit and not just some of our people. We must never rely totally upon one leader. We suffer drastically right now because our dependence is too much upon a Jesse Jackson or a Harold Washington. All of our leaders, if their airplane went down tonight, we would be in a serious state of crisis. The unfortunate thing about the Black community is that we are always in a reactionary posture. We never calculate and predict our movements. What Harold's death represented to us is how dangerous it is to put all your eggs in one basket or to have all your lives in a symbolic leader. Harold was a mayor of the city what we did not own, and all you have to do is drive down the Outer Drive and see all of those buildings and see the skyline and then ask yourself a question, "Is the center of power really on the fifth floor of City Hall, or is it on the 105th floor of John Hancock? Are decisions really made there or are decisions made in those corporate halls where you have batteries of lawyers negotiating on who is really going to get the major contracts and who ultimately benefits even with the Black mayor. Is it Black people? Not really."

THE ROLE OF THE CLERGY IN THE HAROLD WASHINGTON STORY

Jesse Cotton

I choose to say black clergy rather than black church, because we are supposed to keep Church and state separate. The following account is how the black clergy became involved in the political process which eventuated into the election of Harold Washington as mayor of Chicago. And, it is important to note that I had great interest in this process because the city of Chicago is my hometown.

It was on a very hot Sunday morning in August, 1982, during the worship service at Greater Institutional African Methodist Episcopal Church on Chicago's Southside, of which I was the pastor at that time, Harold was there and greeted the congregation. Following his stirring remarks, I predicted to the congregation, that if Congressman Washington were to run for Mayor of Chicago, he would be elected. At that time I did not know of his intentions to urn. A few months later, I was invited to a press conference that he held (Wednesday morning, November 10, 1982), at the Hyde Park Hilton on the Southside of Chicago, I was there. It was at that historic meeting where dozens of black clergy were present to hear Congressman Washington announce his candidacy for Mayor of Chicago.

He made some unusual comments for a Chicago politician. He said that City Hall would have an "Open Door Policy"; he said that he would use the talents of blacks, Latinos, women, poor whites, and others. He wanted to have an inclusive city government.

Following this Press Conference, I was walking along the street with "The Congressman" and I said to him, "If you will give us that kind of city government, I will do all I can to get the support of the black clergy to assure your election." He replied, "Thank you Reverend Cotton, I will need all the help I can get, to fight "THE CHICAGO POLITICAL MACHINE."

After Washington's announcement, several weeks later Richard Daley and Jane Byrne made similar announcements at separate Press Conferences on the Southside with two different groups of black clergy. But I noted that none of these ministers gave their names publicly. I was greatly disturbed that there were no black clergy taking a public stand for Harold Washington. So in the early part of January 1983, I drew up a rough draft of a statement, stating the position of the black church for Harold Washington.

I convened a meeting at Greater Institutional Church at 78th and Indiana Avenue. And at that meeting were the following pastors: Gessel Berry, A. I. Dunlap, Harry Gibson, Gregory Ingram, John W. Jackson, B. Herbert Martin, Al Sampson, Jeremiah Wright and Claude Wyatt. Congressman Washington stopped in at the meeting and gave us his platform and thanked us for our support. This Ad Hoc Committee gave the statement to Reverend Jeremiah Wright to "polish-up" for the press.

A full page statement was paid for and signed by 252 black ministers in the February 12, 1983 edition of the *Chicago Defender* Newspaper, and the February 10, 1983 edition of the *Westside Journal*. These clergy represented 14 different denominations. It is worthy of note here that the statement said the following: "We are public going on record in support of this great leader and we urge All of Chicago to think seriously and to join this growing network of supporters. We have said to him and we say to our constituencies that he not only has our full support, our prayers, and our combined resources; he also has our promise that if he fails to live up to his platform on integrity, we will be the first to condemn him and work for his removal."

Various members of this 252 group of clergy met every week and sometimes twice a week discussing plans as how the black church could become actively involved in this movement. For it was exactly that, a movement and not just another political campaign. I convened all the meetings at Greater Institutional Church. There were a few clergy which gave me frequent support. Some of them were Gregory Ingram, Nathaniel Jarrett, George Walker, Al Sampson, Henry Hardy and Claude Wyatt.

An interesting thing happened at Operation Push Headquarters on the Southside of Chicago in February 1983. Congressman Harold Washington was there and the Reverend Jesse Jackson asked the black clergy present if they would come and place their hand on the head of Congressman Washington, and ask God to so will that he would win the Democratic Primary. The clergy present were Bishop J. Haskell Mayo, Jesse L. Jackson, Henry Hardy and myself. Harold Washington won the primary in April of 1983, as the First Black Mayor of Chicago.

All during the campaign I was the only clergy appointed to the Finance Committee of the Harold Washington for Mayor campaign. The late Bill Berry, my dear friend was the chairperson of this committee. He saw to it that we kept strict account of all funds during this campaign. This group of black clergy for Washington did another unusual thing for the Harold Washington campaign.

We sponsored a PRAYER BREAKFAST, which was ecumenical. It was on Saturday, April 9, 1983, at the well-known Palmer House in downtown Chicago. In attendance were over one thousand persons. We raised over $16,000 for the Washington campaign.

After Congressman Harold Washington was elected Mayor a few days later, he did the unusual, he invited all of the losing candidates to "A Unity Luncheon" and I was honored to be invited. I took along with me, my bishop, the Rt. Reverend Hubert N. Robinson. Seated at the Mayor's table was Bishop Robinson, Jane

Byrne, Richard Daley and Judge Epton, the brother of Bernard Upton (The Republican Candidate). At that time no one knew why Bernard Epton did not show, but I had first hand information from a nurse at Michael Reese Hospital. Bernard Epton had been admitted, very quietly, as a patient there. I whispered this to Mayor Washington and he told me to give this information to one of his assistants, which I did.

On April 29, 1983, I pronounced the benediction at the Inauguration of Harold Washington. My prayer want as follows: ETERNAL GOD, THE GOD OF ALL HUMANKIND, WE COME TO THE CLOSE OF THIS HISTORIC OCCASION WITH BOWED HEADS AND CONTRITE HEARTS ASKING THAT THOU WOULDEST ANOINT THY SERVANT HAROLD WASHINGTON WITH THY CHOICE BENEDICTION. DISMISS US FROM THIS PLACE, GIVING US THE SINCERE DESIRE TO MAKE OUR GREAT CITY BETTER THAN EVER, UNDER THE LEADERSHIP OF OUR NEW MAYOR. WE GATHER FROM VARIOUS RELIGIOUS PERSUASIONS, CLASPING THE HAND OF OUR NEIGHBOR NOW, AS A SYMBOL OF OUR WILLINGNESS TO CREATE TOGETHER, A NEW WHOLESOME IMAGE OF CHICAGO, FOR ALL THE WORLD TO EMULATE. HIDE US NOW UNDER THE SHADOW OF THY PROTECTIVE WINGS AS WE GO AND MAY WE ALL KNOW THY PEACE AND LOVE THAT PASSETH ALL HUMAN UNDERSTANDING. AMEN!"

After the prayer, I then congratulated the Mayor. He said, "You predicted this for me."

Well, once he became mayor, the old machine at City Hall had lined up fight him every step of the way. Again I wanted to do something through the church to aid our new mayor, because there was so much tension. So I organized an Ecumenical-Interracial/Interfaith service, which was designed to assist in uniting the City Council. Such a service was held at Quinn Chapel African

Methodist Episcopal Church (the oldest black church in Chicago). Gregory Ingram was serving as the host pastor. At this Ecumenical Prayer Service, Mayor Washington was present, along with four members of the City Council. However, I invited all 50 members of the City Council. The four members present were Timothy Evans, Eugene Sawyer, Allan Streeter and one white alderman, Lawrence Bloom. This suggested that the City Council was not ready for unity nor reform.

About mid-way through his first term Mayor Washington wanted to follow through on more of his campaign promises to the Black Clergy, so he appointed a Blue Ribbon Committee to draw up an ordinance for Ethics in City Government. There were about a dozen persons including aldermen, lawyers, professors and clergy; I was the only Black Clergy on it and the only Black Alderman was Timothy Evans. We worked diligently on that ordinance for 18 months, sometimes every week. Of course such an ordinance was strongly opposed by the Ole Machine in City Hall. The ordinance was finally passed by the City Council about a year ago. It was September 29, 1983; I invited Mayor Washington to be the Guest Speaker in Toronto, Canada, at the Centennial Celebration of the African Methodist Episcopal Church. It was fitting that he speak because his father and grandfather were both ministers in Chicago in the African Methodist Episcopal Church. I had the honor of presenting him.

I think one of the highest honors paid me by my late friend, was when he spoke on Sunday Morning, February 19, 1984, at Greater Institutional African Methodist Episcopal Church, at which time he told the congregation of our close friendship. Following that service he came to my home and my dear wife (Thelma Cotton) prepared dinner at which time we exchange ideas as to how the Black Clergy could continue to assist him in the background and not on the City's payroll.

In the Spring of 1986, some things were occurring that disturbed me connected with my friend Mayor Harold Washington. The

Press, it appeared was trying to undermine his administration, so again I called the leading Black Clergy of our city together and gave them a draft of a statement that I prayed that they would approve of and publish. The ministers approved the Press Release, with very few changes and over 150 Black Clergy again signed their names to it. It was published in the *Chicago Defender* Saturday, April 5, 1986, entitled: "The Black Clergy Reaffirms Their Stand for Mayor Harold Washington." On that same morning, I had the Mayor's private telephone number at home, which he gave me, so I called him to tell him about it, and he said, "Yes, Rev. I saw it and believe me when I say that it has made my day, especially after the way the Press has been treating me lately. Please express my appreciation to all of the ministers for their continued support."

In closing may I make this observation: The Black Church should never divorce itself from politics. We should develop, educate, train and encourage young Black Christians to enter the field of politics for we need politicians like the late Mayor Harold Washington, who will stand for ethics, even in politics. If we as Black Pastors cry out loud from our pulpits for our people to seek out and support worthy Black candidates for political office, for in the long run we shall reap many benefits like the Blacks in City Hall of Chicago. If we are to have true Black Power in this country, it must come through the ballot box.

HAROLD WASHINGTON AND THE POLITICS OF INCLUSIVENESS

THE BLACK CHURCH THEN AND NOW

Harry B. Gibson

Well, I have to begin by saying that I came to Chicago just before the question of a black mayoral candidate was being discussed. And I would say that I came back at a most exciting time. I am very glad that I did. I had been in Chicago during the 1950s and 60s. I went to New York to work for The Board of Global Ministries of the United Methodist Church. After staying in New York for several years, I returned in 1981, just before the campaign began. So I had that background. I would have to say that the period of time between 1982 and 1987, were some of the most exciting years of my life and in my ministry. I cannot separate the two. I perceived the political process leading to the mayoralty of Harold Washington. I felt that involvement in the campaign was integral to the ministry and mission of the black church. I suddenly realized that I was involved in what can be described as a crusade, rather than a campaign.

It went far beyond the political dimensions and took upon itself religious dimensions as well. It indeed became a crusade because we felt that we were dealing, at rock bottom, with what human life and its fulfillment was all about. This becomes more apparent when one of the history of politics in Chicago.

As I reflect on my experiences in Chicago, beginning in 1955, when I served as pastor of Gorham United Methodist Church, we had very few political activists in the city. We had "plantation politics," the rule which governed all that we did in this city. And Chicago has always been a politically oriented city. I began to see in the Harold Washington movement the possibility of reversing "plantation politics" in Chicago. "Plantation politics" was not based on a participatory form of government, in terms of blacks, women and other oppressed minority social groups. It was based on tokenism, at best. A few people were chosen by the political machine to represent minority groups. Minority persons viewed an altogether different spirit coming out of the political experience and leadership, which Harold Washington was providing. When I began to work more closely with Harold Washington, I became convinced that his mayoralty marked a new era for all people of Chicago.

In one of the first conversations I had with Harold Washington at St. Mark United Methodist Church when he was trying to really make the decision to run for mayor, I confronted him with the basic question. I asked, "Are you serious? Because the community is not willing to mobilize its forces if you are not serious." He said, "Yes, I am now beginning to be serious about this. I want to be Mayor of Chicago." With that out of the way, he went on to confide in me. He pointed out that he didn't want to be mayor of just one particular interest social group. He said, I would like to be mayor of all the people. I could see that he was a politically astute person. He knew how to count numbers politically very well. And he knew how to be inclusive politically. However, I think this inclusive aspect was just beginning to bear fruit when he began his second term.

Politically and pragmatically, he had to be elected principally by the black community. So it was a kind of compromise with himself. He said, if that's the only way to be elected, then, so be it. But it is obvious that he was moving away from the proposition that we wanted to serve just one segment of the community at the exclusion of other social groups. In fact, it is clear to me that in the very inception of Harold Washington's effort to run for Mayor, his orientation was to be a representative of all the people.

Notwithstanding, in spite of the editorials, including television, radio, journals and newspapers that attempted to portray his campaign as only representative of the black community, Harold Washington wanted to be mayor of all the people. He attempted to be honest, fair and just with all of the people. Although being black was an asset to Harold Washington, his big agenda was an effort to bring all ethnic social groups together.

This also was the agenda of the black community in the 1950s and 1960s; but Mayor Daley, for example, refused to respond to it. And other mayors that followed Daley didn't respond. They would maneuver the various communities for political reasons; but for someone who was committed to the socio-economic advancement of persons, regardless of race or ethnic background, I saw in Harold Washington the first mayor of the city of Chicago who really came with that kind of agenda.

As far back as I can remember, including all that I have read about the black church historically,m it has always been inclusive. I went to a black college, which was an arm of the black church (Philander Smith College). Black colleges always had mixed faculties, and mixed scholars from other ethnic/racial backgrounds. These scholars and faculties have always been accepted on our college campuses. The student body was open for enrollment to others and these were church-related campuses, colleges and universities. Inclusiveness has always been the modus operandi of black colleges and universities. And, it is important to note that the spirit of inclusiveness in the black community was born in the black church. The United Methodist Church, which was first the Methodist Church and later the Methodist Episcopal Church, has always had a philosophy of inclusiveness; although it hasn't practiced it. So then the black church never excluded any ethnic social groups from its membership.

In my judgment, the black church has always been a pioneering institution for inclusiveness. And even during those times when the black church was charged with being too radical or too far to the left, in terms of pushing for the rights of black people, at no time can I recall in the history of the black church did we say that this was done by denying the rights of other people.

One of the crucial elements in the very beginning, as we sought to make the contacts that were necessary to get the black religious committee together in support of Harold Washington's campaign, was the manner in which some sectors of the black religious leadership in Chicago had related to previous mayoralty administrations. This was a delicate matter. But we challenged them and began to make inroads and especially after the primary victory to enlist the aid of a large number of those who had that kind of background, and now we were beginning to mobilize into an army that would not be defeated.

Some of the survival in the black community depended on how leadership related to the mayor and other political leaders in the city, and not just for personal gain (although they included that), but also as ministers attempted t find jobs and economic improvement for members in the black community at-large. So there was this history of that kind of relationship to the Daley administration, and to the Byrne administration (and we were still in the Byrne administration).

I think in all fairness, it could be said that for some of these religious leaders especially, who were related to the former administration they were trying to survive. They were trying to help their people survive. And if they could get political jobs or socioeconomic advancement of any kind, they felt this was the best they could do under the existing circumstances. When they saw the possibility of not only surviving but reaching with hope toward becoming a part of a crusade for justice for all people, they began to lose their reluctance and began to join the crusade to bring in a new era in the city of Chicago.

I recall very distinctly in the fall, one cold, clear wintry night in 1982, prior to the campaign and before even anybody was really serious about electing a black mayor, Lou Palmer invited Jeremiah Wright and myself to his radio broadcast at 10 o'clock at night to appear on his talk show. The purpose was to discuss the role of religion and the black church in politics and in the community at-large. We began to answer the questions as they came in on the telephone, and we discussed the possibility of electing a black mayor and what a role the black church could play in such an endeavor.

People began to get excited about two preachers coming out there that night to talk about the black church being really concerned enough about the plight of black people to be in the leadership of such a movement. I will never forget that experience. It was so new an experience that we laughed among ourselves wondering if it was safe to go outside in the dark where we had parked our cars, because such an event was unheard of at that particular time in Chicago.

It was also exciting to involve clergy. The first known meeting of clergy was held the wintertime of 1982, with Harold Washington (then a Congressman). It was a meeting for the black clergy held at St. Mark United Methodist Church to discuss the possibilities of our support to Congressman Washington as the mayor of Chicago. We set a public meeting on that particular day. And in January of 1983, we had a public meeting, which was one of the first mass meetings in the city focus on the Harold Washington campaign.

Earlier I alluded to the excitement I felt at being a part of this movement. It was certainly an honor and I was pleased to respond to the invitation to serve on the steering committee, a committee composed of about fifteen to twenty people, who monitored the total campaign from its inception to victory. There were two or three other pastors on the steering committee. Claude Wyatt and I served as co-chairpersons of the religious community component. The clergy that served with us were Donald Parson and Morales, from the Hispanic community. Jesse Cotton served on the

Finance Committee; he played an essential role in the campaign from almost the very beginning.

Now one of the projects which generated a lot of excitement, in terms of participation as a religious community, centered around an ad which appeared before the primary election. I saw in the *Chicago Defender* one morning at breakfast, a full page ad, which had been taken out by one of our leading black clergy persons on behalf of Jane Byrne as the campaign began. My oatmeal went everywhere and I forgot that I was a preacher at the moment. We had had two or three meetings of the steering committee, and I began to wonder what we could do to respond to the ad. In the meantime, the paper was carrying every two or three days, pictures of Jane Byrne meeting with ministers. They could only show three or four figures and then feature Jane Byrne, and they would say, "thirty to forty" ministers meet with Jane Byrne." And everybody began to wonder who were these ministers? Where did they get the numbers? Were they authentic?

I conceived the notion, and took it to our steering committee on the following Saturday, of having an ad put in the newspaper sponsored by the religious leadership in the Harold Washington campaign. After approval of the idea was given by the steering committee, we went to work, Claude Wyatt and myself, contacting ministers throughout the city. They came together and endorsed the idea. This was indeed a significant development in the Harold Washington campaign.

This was in 1983. It was in the first campaign and it took place before the primary. This is very essential, because others joined us after the primary. I think the ad was very important. There was a kind of "snowballing" after the primary.

The very first significant gathering that really made the Washington campaign appear to be serious was that gathering at the Pavilion, just before the primary. The Pavilion seats thousands of people. There wasn't an empty seat and some people were standing. Up to that time, we did not know what kind of crowd we could gather. It was a rainy Sunday afternoon, and there were rumors that if you parked your car around there, certain forces in the community would employ the gangs to damage the cars. In spite of all this, the place was packed. It was at the Pavilion that I was asked to present the ad "THE BLACK CHURCH IS NOT FOR SALE." I read the ad with some comments, so the whole community would know where this portion of the leadership stood. By this time, this leadership represented a significant portion of the religious community.

The meeting at the Pavilion took place on a snowy Sunday afternoon in February of 1983. The crowd was overwhelming in numbers. In fact, there was standing room only. With Jesse Cotton standing by my side I read the challenge to the then Congressman Washington indicating that "we will be the first to hold you accountable if the spirit of this document is violated."

I pointed out that at a crucial time in the beginning days of the 1983 primary campaign, non-black candidates staged meetings with groups of un-named black ministers. These meetings were reported in the media as being supportive of Jane Byrne. Utilizing the platform of PUSH (People United to Serve Humanity), I suggested to the black clergy of Chicago to "sign on the line," meaning the appeal was to get substantive support for the Washington campaign. some 250 clergy from a broad ecumenical base signed the historic full page ad, THE BLACK CHURCH IS NOT FOR SALE."

HISTORICAL OVERVIEW OF HAROLD WASHINGTON'S POLITICAL CAREER

BEGINNINGS OF "THE MAN-THE MESSAGE-THE MOVEMENT"

John R. Porter

My acquaintance with Harold Washington's political career started in 1967 when he was a state representative. His office was first located on 63rd and Peoria; he later moved to 63rd and Wentworth. At that time Charles Freeman and Harold Washington were partners in law, located approximately one block from Christ United Methodist Church. Because Charles Freeman served as my personal attorney, it gave me immediate access to both Charles Freeman and Harold Washington. I visited their office quite frequently for counsel and advice, because I was involved quite heavily in social activism.

I participated in leading protests and demonstrations against police brutality in the community, unemployment, discrimination against blacks, the sale of bad meat to blacks by white merchants, and other problems. And, it appeared that, at least, once a week I was either protesting or getting arrested for leading a demonstration. Because the news media frequently carried stories about social activists and civil rights leaders that were characterized as "trouble makers," it made my ministry extremely vulnerable. This meant that I needed constant counsel from Charles Freeman and Harold Washington.

I was then serving as founder and President of the Chicago chapter of the Southern Christian Leadership Conference. It was started in 1964, as the first of Martin Luther King's organizations in Chicago. Many clergy in Chicago were afraid to start the organization. Martin Luther King had approached other clergy to consider starting a chapter but many feared repercussions from Mayor Daley. This is to say a large percentage of clergy in the city had economic ties to what was then known as the Daley political machine. It is a component which helps us to understand the extensiveness of the Daley machine.

Although when Harold Washington launched his political career the political machine was still in place, his independent spirit would not allow him to accept what the political machine attempted to offer him. I often had conversations with Harold Washington in the late 1960s about the value of independence and commitment. He had many questions about the plight of oppressed minority social groups and their need for independence. In fact, many times he said to me, "Reverend Porter, I see that you are marching again, keep it up, because we need it." I knew, however, at the time, he was emphathetic, but could not come out publicly and take a position.

Harold Washington soon became a state senator. He was slowly emerging at his zenith as a lawyer, state representative and state senator. In 1977, he ran against Mayor Daley and he lost. But he demonstrated a sense of strong independence. In the early 1970s, Dick Newhouse and others were led by Harold Washington in introducing a bill to make the birthday of Martin Luther King, Jr. a state holiday. He eventually succeeded in accomplishing it.

In the early 1980s, Lou Palmer, who is a symbol of political strength in the black community, convened a meeting at his home for the purpose of beginning conversations about the future of black politics in the city of Chicago. About twenty persons were in attendance. Vernon Jarrett was among those present. All of us were becoming increasing aware of the need for black political empowerment. As we discussed together the need to identify a potential black candidate for the office of mayor certain criteria were considered. The first criterion dealt with freedom. The person selected needed to have a strong desire for oppressed social groups to achieve independence politically, socially and economically. The person could not afford to be controlled by the political machine. In fact, we wanted someone with the political sensitivity and knowledge to lead the community in the direction of dismantling the political machine.

Secondly, the person had to have a profound sense of integrity. The person needed to be his/her own person. We needed someone with a willingness to sacrifice and suffer for the cause of liberation, if necessary. Thirdly, in addition to being qualified, competent and committed, the person needed to have undying love for the oppressed victims of sexism, racism, classism and imperialism. We didn't realize at the time that these criteria were interwoven into the shaping of Harold Washington as the future mayor of Chicago, which was to take place approximately eight years later. Fortunately, I was a part of the process from the beginning.

The Chicago political machine had been in power since 1922. It had worked against blacks and other minority social groups for more than sixty years. There were about three generations of blacks, living and dead, that were victims of this political. It was the last of the big old political machines. Other political machines throughout the country were over. The Boston political machine was gone; the same thing can be said about Memphis, New York, Missouri, Cleveland and Los Angeles. The last one was Chicago. It represented the last bastion of resistance against black political empowerment.

When the black community began to think seriously about the possibility of choosing a candidate to run for mayor, it was decided that we would do two things. First, we checked with Harold Washington to see whether he was interested in being considered. He was an obvious choice because he knew the political machine. Also, he had demonstrated a strong sense of political independence. He had run against Mayor Daley. He had succeeded in making the birthday of Martin Luther King, Jr. a holiday. He made public statements about how the political machine's domination of blacks and other minority social groups needed to stop. He impregnated upon our minds the need to come together in unity. Therefore, we called Harold Washington into our meetings for interviews and discussions.

And the second thing we wanted to do was to hold a plebiscite and engage as many citizens as possible in selecting at least twenty names of outstanding persons to be considered as potential candidates. Then the black community would vote on which candidate they would want for mayor. The community set the criteria, educated itself to the political process and raised its level of consciousness; and I think between sixty to one hundred thousand people participated in the event. They asked Harold Washington whether he would consider running for the office of mayor of the city. Initially, Washington hesitated, because he was a Congressman; he was quite satisfied with what he was doing; he was very effective. He did not see any reason to leave that office for what he knew would be a hard fight and what could end up in another defeat. For the political machine was still formidable after Daley. At that time Jane Byrne was in control of it. She had won it in 1979, from Blandic. She had grown in popularity among white voters, a number of black voters and female voters. And Blacks had become very dissatisfied with Jane Byrne because she had replaced two blacks on the Board of Education with two white women from the Southwest community, and she had done other things to indicate her disdain with the black community.

So what we did was to ask Harold Washington three or four questions. First, would he consider running? No, he replied. He didn't think he wanted to consider running. Secondly, we asked him did he consider that he was qualified for the office. He responded affirmatively. He felt, unquestionable, that he was qualified and that he could do the job well. Thirdly, we wanted to know whether there was anything in his past or lifestyle that the public could use against him.

Then we moved to the level of having the plebiscite. We had a conference on politics at Malcolm X College. It had to do with black politics and the preparation for the possible election of a black mayor. Hardly anybody, at that time, believed the election of a black mayor was possible. Many people felt that we were not ready; they didn't think that we could find a viable candidate. Also, they didn't think that we could get the amount of votes that we needed. We needed approximately four hundred thousand black votes; and we needed another one hundred fifty thousand votes from whites, hispanics and asians.

The feeling was that a lot of people really didn't know much about Harold Washington. Because during the early phase of his political career he was not always in the headlines, and when he was in the headlines, it was in the Chicago Defender. He didn't have a lot of visibility in the Sun Times, the Chicago Tribune, Daily News and magazines. But we knew he would soon get visibility and recognition because he was one of the most articulate persons being considered. And, he had a great sense of humor. He had tremendous oratory. He was as good as Jesse Jackson and almost as good as Martin Luther King, Jr. He had an excellent grasp of facts as they relate to current issues. He was well read. In fact, he would read at least a book each week. He was an intellectual politician. He was well feasted on ideas. He was married to politics. I would even say that he was the consummation of politics.

After the conference at Malcolm X College we came out with a plebiscite. The people, overwhelmingly, wanted Harold Washington. We went to him again and said, "The people want you, Harold." We met with him again and he said, "I tell you what, register fifty thousand new voters by October of 1982, and I will seriously consider running for the office of mayor. I think I will file."

Well, in early October of 1982, we had registered one hundred and twenty-five thousand new voters, with a goal that Harold

Washington accepted. We registered another eighty thousand new voters in January of 1983. The election was in March of 1983. Now, Harold Washington had accepted our offer.

It is important to note that November 10, 1982, at the Hyde Park Hilton Hotel, Harold Washington made his announcement. Persons were in attendance from all walks of life. The crowd consisted of over fifteen hundred people. I was present, along with over one hundred other clergy. It was decided during the deliberations that a prayer was needed before the announcement. It was most unusual to request prayer to be rendered at a political gathering. In fact, the news media mentioned that a political gathering it was unusual to ask a minister to give a prayer. But they didn't understand the Black experience. They didn't understand just how interdependent and tightly interwoven politics, business, education, fraternities, sororities and other organizations are within the infrastructure of the black church.

The black church is the mother of these establishments in the black community. Politics in the black community cannot succeed without the black church and the black preacher. So they looked in the crowd and there was Jesse Jackson, Father George Clements and whole lot of people. And they reached over and said, "John Porter, come on up and pray as the mayor comes in."

And so the spirit of God came to me and somewhere in the prayer I started mentioning the phrase, "THE MANE, THE MOMENT, AND THE MOVEMENT." My thinking was that the three had come together into a creative synthesis. God had a hold on them. And God has given us a new King and this new King had come, not to rule over us as a despot; but rather, he had come to guide us out of political slavery in the city. He had come to guide us out of sixty-two years of plantation politics. He had come to give the masses, those live, dead, and even unborn, a sense of new hope. He had come to galvanize, not only this city, but this nation.

And I knew that if Harold Washington falls in line with the drumbeat of social justice, as reflected in the lives of Martin Luther King, Jr., W. E. B. DuBois, Carter G. Woodson, Frederick Douglass and others, he would go down in history as one of the greatest leaders our people have produced. And not only that, but he would be a King for all the people, black and white, yellow, red, male and female, and others. All segments of the city would be blessed because of Harold Washington's decision. And I prayed for God to crown him with righteousness and justice, and to hold him up and send him forth like a lightening bolt to free his people. My prayer was made in Jesus' name, Amen.

The crowd was so excited that it was as if it lifted Harold Washington up on wings. It was almost like he floated in the crowd. I saw tears in the eyes of clergy and lay persons. This was the case for both black and white persons. I saw little ladies shaking their heads in celebration. I saw them savoring and experiencing this moment. I looked in Lou Palmers's face and saw great intentionality. Because Lou Palmer contributed so much to shape this moment. The forces of history had given birth to a new idea manifested in the legacy of Harold Washington. Jesse Jackson, with his public relation skills, helped to give visibility to the moment. It was a moment that was eclectic. It was a synergistic moment in which larger forces of history were at work.

History had seized Harold Washington. He was already a great person, but his decision made him even a greater person in the eyes of the masses. It made him a servant of God and a leader of all people. He pulled off something that had never been done before in the city of Chicago. And that is why he was endeared by the masses. First of all, he made it a point to not only fall in love with politics, but he loved people at the grassroots level. He loved people from every walk of life.

And it was after his announcement that we went to work to get some more people registered. My focus was in the 15th through the 17th wards. I became one of his representatives. In the Englewood area I became a campaign strategist.

So, basically, Harold Washington was married to politics. He was the consummate politician. He decided to marry politics in order to arrive at the point where he could have a mastery and control of the political process. And the black church was his base.

Now there were some blacks who were alienated from the black church because they didn't understand its significance until Harold Washington was elected. They, they began to see. The masses of people in the black church fell in love with Harold Washington. And he made it a point to visit the smallest to the largest black church.

While Harold Washington was in office, he brought in more women, blacks, hispanics, poor whites and other oppressed persons in positions of leadership than any mayor in the history of Chicago. When one looks at the infrastructure of the city's departments, such as the Police Department, Department of Human Service, Department of Public Works, Housing Department, O'Hare Airport, and so forth, one sees more deputies and commissioners from minority social groups than ever before in the history of the Chicago city government. He produced a reform movement. The significant thing is that he became the movement. Therefore, nobody could get elected finally without Harold's endorsement. He became indigenized in the psyche of the people. But, of course, this has some limitations that need to be considered.

The limitations have to do with the problem of succession in the black community. We have a real problem of leadership succession. However, this is a problem which has haunted us ever since slavery. We've always had that one charismatic leader, the one out front. But what happens when such a leader dies or is killed?

I think we have to take the present younger generation and train them to be leaders. We need a sense of collective leadership. No longer can we afford to invest in one single leader. We must become more collective in our approach to leadership. The challenge is for us to think more collectively than individualistically. Now, take a look at the problem of leadership since the death of Harold Washington. There is a scramble to replace him. Harold Washington inherited the problem that many black leaders have. As a charismatic individual leader, who because of being accomplished and developed intellectually, simply did not take the time to train and prepare others who could come after him. Even his closest associates did not know what the plan was, in terms of leadership succession. And even those who had known him for years did not know what the next turn in the road would be or where we ought to go.

So, I think that in summary, we must collectivize the movement. The movement must come together. The movement must be truly indigenized and owned by the masses, which includes blacks, whites, hispanics, and others.

REMEMBERING HAROLD WASHINGTON

Eddie L. Robinson

Black people in the United Methodist Church have historically understood that the gospel message of salvation included more than life in the hereafter. The message of hope proclaimed by Jesus must also have some application to the existential situation of people. One needs only to recall the ministry of the late Charles Albert Tindley, noted composer and Methodist preacher. Not only did people hear a dynamic word from the pulpit of Tindley Temple in Philadelphia, but through the various outreach ministries of the church they also experienced the incarnation of that word of hope from on high. The hungry were fed, the naked were clothed, the forgotten were remembered, the rejected were embraced and the good news was preached. A more contemporary example of this incarnated work, came to life in the church's outreach ministries through the work of Chicago Black Methodists for Church Renewals' (BMCR) Congregational Outreach and Empowerment Committee. Through COEC, local United Methodist congregations are provided resources to support such ministries as food pantries and tutorial programs. These outreach programs help the church say that people are of value; both soul and situation are our concern.

Our church discipline reminds us that in the congregational settings, we are the Church made visible to the world. Through what we say and what we do we convince the world -- our local communities -- of the reality of the gospel or leave it unconvinced. We cannot evade this task; either we are faithful as a witnessing and serving community, or we lose our vitality and impact. When BMCR was founded in Cincinnati nearly 20 years ago the message was delivered by Dr. Earnest Smith of our Board of Church Society in Washington, concluded with a challenge that "From this day forward our dedication must be deep, our commitment sure and our actions certain. God's work and way are contemporary in every age. There is no waiting for tomorrow.... Our time under God is now!" This is our rallying cry even today. We are called to make the best out of whatever situation our people are in . The ministries provided by Delaney in Gary, Indiana through the former Stewart House, were yet another expression of the commitment of black Methodists to share the good news in every age. And, the involvement of Black clergy in the movement to elect Harold Washington follows this ceaseless, timeless, expression of care and commitment that is characteristic of Black United Methodists.

The Methodist Episcopal Church is not a 'Johnny-come-lately' to the movement to help change the condition of Black folk. After the Civil War, the church founded the Black colleges such as Dillard, Clark and Meharrg. Our hospitals and schools -- some readily identified by the employment of Wesleyan or Methodist in their name -- suggest that we are concerned with the whole person, not just the spiritual needs. God's claim on us and Christ's call to us precludes us from being concerned with just one dimension of life. This is the legacy of the Wesleyan experience in America. We have tried to reach out to touch the wounds to the human predicament caused by blows from the many different forces which attack people from all sides.

The Harold Washington campaign represents the political dimension of Black United Method's commitment to uplift the lives of our people. In Chicago, Blacks had long suffered from a disenfranchisement from the political process. It was not that we didn't vote because we did, in large, predictable numbers. We just didn't have much of a say so in the decision making. For the most part, City Hall ignored Blacks. Our elected officials, such as they were, were controlled by the Democratic Machine and our people felt voiceless. This hung heavy on their minds during the week and came with them to church on Sunday morning. A concerned pastor would have to address this issue and concern of the people. When Harold's campaign started, the clergy were simply working to help alleviate a particular problem experienced by their constituencies. That is what one would expect from their pastor; to try to do something about something. However, when the church moves to act in the name of Jesus, the congregation will view what happens in a context and perspective that is different from persons who may not be a part of a church community. The church sees a divine response taking root and shape. God had inclined his ear, heard the prayers and supplications of his people and was now acting. The election of the mayor had a divine imprint on it. We saw and felt in the victory celebration the same sense of excitement and joy Israel experienced when they were delivered out of Egypt.

Faith has taught us that the workings of Providence are a mystery. We even sing "God works in mysterious ways his wonders to perform." So it was that when Harold passed so suddenly the query of people was again similar to Israel's concern when Moses died, "Who will lead us?" People wanted to know what would become of the movement, the coalition and the hopes and dreams of a newly delivered community. Israel had walked through a wilderness experience and Blacks in Chicago had a wilderness factor to contend with too. For all practical purposes, politics in Chicago had been for us a barren wilderness until the advent of Harold's election. But that brief moment of celebration seemed to be so quickly dashed on the rocks of the valley of death until we again remembered that God did indeed raise up a Joshua to lead the people through the conquest and settlement of Canaan. At the moment we don't know who that person is but we do know that all is not lost. This is the message that comes from our pulpits even now.

Early in Harold's campaign, it was necessary for people in the pews to meet the candidate. Harold was not then a household word. People in his congressional district knew him and others knew of him. He had once mounted, in the 70s, an ill-fated run at the Fifth floor and there may have been folk who remembered the name but most folk didn't have the slightest idea of who Harold Washington was. Through a series of rallies in churches around the city, Harold was able to establish and re-establish his presence in the community as a serious mayoral candidate. Prior to the campaign if you stopped the average person on 47th Street and asked them who was "Harold" most folk would think that you were asking about the man who owned the chain of chicken shacks. It wa through the congregational meeting process where he was able to share his message to people from all walks of life that Harold's name was catapulted into the forefront of the community's consciousness. The United Methodist Church played a vital role in his emergence as a factor to be reckoned with. Dr. John Porter of Christ United Methodist Church in Englewood, in an early meeting of the campaign, spoke of "the man, the moment and the message" coming together. That was a prophetic word and it came from a United Methodist preacher. It came, as it were, long before a whole lot of other folk decided to get on the bank wagon.

Harold understood that the church is the most powerful institution in the Black community. If he was serious in his candidacy, he would need the support of the church. He frequented churches. His father was a minister. He grew up in a church. He belonged to Progressive Community Church. Harold knew of the strength of the church and was more than willing to incorporate it's strengths into his campaign. Politicians have also come to the church looking for votes. His opponents did it and candidates before them. That's part of the election strategy. Go to church, meet the people, make a donation, make a speech and then make an exit until the next campaign. Harold, however, didn't have money. He had himself and that was a better offering. He gave himself to the people and, in turn, the people gave him City Hall along with their hopes and dreams that things would be different. And somewhere in the process, you could year the faint melody of our foreparents saying "Walk together children, don't get weary, there's a great camp meeting in the promise land."

Before Harold, Blacks had been rebuked by the Democratic Machine. His predecessor did not do well by our people. Nor did her predecessor. Or Daley either. But with Harold, there was a sense that things would be different. We now not only had access to the Fifth Floor, one of us sat behind the desk. That was the "bright side somewhere" of our heritage. Blacks began to believe in the power of resident in our vote. This did not happen, however overnight.

Politics centers around vested interests. And, around town there were Black folk whose vested interests were not initially in the Washington campaign. Their political loyalties and allegiances were in another quarter. Plantation politics ruled and for some, their political livelihood meant that they could not support Harold. Traditionally, there are several wards who support and vote for whoever the Machine promoted as its candidate. On election days, the voter turnout and support for those candidates were almost predictable. They were assured their victory before the election booths opened. Harold Washington's campaign gave the people a voice in the matter and they spoke rather convincingly.

Looking back, it's a wonder that our folk didn't speak earlier. Yet, we know why folk did not speak. They felt it really didn't matter. The average person felt a sense of hopelessness and alienation from City Hall until Harold came along and people could identify with him. One of us; somebody from the block who spoke the language of the people calling the people to speak. They sense his love and concern for them and spoke that he should go to City Hall.

Jesus said, "I come that you might have life and have it more abundantly," and in Harold's victory we discovered anew what the abundant life could be. That we cared for one another, that we worked and struggled together and tried to make this place a little different than it was when we came here. Harold's arrival on the Fifth Floor lifted the expectations of people so that politics in Chicago will never be quite the same again. Folk will try to maintain the status quo of yesterday but the new spirit says that "this too will pass." Martin's words are appropriate to the legacy of Harold Washington. He told us that he ha been to the mountaintop and saw the promised land. It is now up to us to claim it and to see Harold on the other side.

THE ROLE OF WOMEN IN THE HAROLD WASHINGTON STORY

Addie Wyatt

I have been a political activist for many years prior to Harold Washington's election as a state representative/senator and congressman of the United States. But this particular time something very strange happened to me. I was commuting, because of my job, from Washington, D.C. to Chicago. But one Monday morning when I began to get myself ready to return to Washington, D.C., God spoke to me and said that I should read the fourth chapter of Judges. I was in a hurry, trying to pack and get on over to the plane so that I could get back to my office; I was due there at 10 o'clock in the morning. But as I continued to try to ignore it, I still got this warning again to read the fourth chapter of Judges. And after I read it the second time something spoke to me and said to go to Harold Washington's office and tell him he is to be the Mayor of Chicago.

Now this was somewhat embarrassing to me because how do you go and say to the congressman, God has sent me to tell you, you're supposed to be the Mayor of the City of Chicago. So I put my Bible down and picked up my bags. And I proceeded to get in my car and go to Congressman Washington's office. I was somewhat embarrassed. I was hoping he wouldn't even be there. Because I didn't know how I would really tell him that God told me to come to him. And when I went there, I asked for him at the reception desk; and the young women stalled and that was relieving me because I knew he wasn't there. And finally, she said just a moment. He then called and said, "let her in."

I went and spoke in a hurry. I had a red Bible with me. And I said, "Congressman, God told me to come over and tell you that you are to be the Mayor of the City of Chicago." He laughed. He called me angel. He said, "Angel, you're the one who should be mayor of the City of Chicago." I said, "but that isn't what God told me." He laughed and he laughed. I said, "Now, God told me to tell you to read the fourth chapter of Judges. You'll read that story about Deborah and Barach." I said, "God knows that we don't have what it takes to win. God knows that we have no money. But what God is saying to us is that God will go before he and God is going to deliver this city into our hands and we will not be able to take credit for it. We'll have to say, 'Only God did this for us.'" He laughed. And I said, "Well, when you get a chance you just read it and I'm now going and I will be able to say I told you so."

Now that was a strange thing to happen to me. I then went back an took a plane into Washington, D.C. still feeling very foolish. And within a couple of days, I got a call from Bill Barry and several of them asking if I would come back into Chicago within a couple of weeks. I said, "back into Chicago?" They wanted me to work with the Women for Harold Washington. He had meetings with several of our people. He had consented to run despite the fact that he was content to be the congressman. And I said to him, "I know you are an excellent congressman, because everybody I meet in Washington thanks us for sending you to Congress."

But after several weeks, he began meeting with some of our key people, those who formed our political coalition, labor, community organization and the church. And he said to them, if you really get a good vote out this would be a good indication that the people are serious. And we told him, we have the people; we just didn't have the candidate. And that's where we were seeking for. And I committed myself to come in to pull together the women. And I said to them, if I'm permitted to pull together black women, white women, hispanic women, asian women, native American, all women together, that it would constitute a winnable coalition. And with that kind of coalition and the direction of God, we can win. We had no money. We were trying to get some leaflets out. Many people doubted that he could be elected. Black and white figured it was a hopeless situation. But there were some black Congressmen who felt that if we took a dare, then we could do it.

I was so confident because I was really going with the word of God that was deep within my heart. I was beginning to understand more and more what God was saying. Now, really I must tell you that whenever I work on a committee or anything, it is really at the direction of God, because I hate to lose. And I think with God, we're winners.

But to make a long story short, we called a meeting together; several of us met together -- women, white, black, hispanic and others. The meeting consisted of approximately 100 women. We wanted to sample their interests and see how they felt about it. We wanted to know if they were willing to raise money. And we held that meeting on the 20th of December in 1982, at the Conrad Hilton in a little small group, just enough for 100 women. And that night, when we came in, there were over 200 women all out in the hallways and corridors. And the enthusiasm was so great; but I paused to tell them why I got on board. I wanted to tell them for encouragement to those who would accept the task. And I started telling them about Deborah and Barach.

And I said to the, because of this it may be rough going. We may not have money. We may not have many things, but I'm not dealing with what we have, I'm dealing with what God has. God is moving with us and on our behalf. Some of them said, now does she have to start preaching. And I said well, you know, it may be different for some people. I just have to let you know where I stand. Some women become so discouraged. I said, I'll be standing right here to try to lift us up and I hope you will do the same. There were some in that room who were nodding because they knew and could bear witness to what we were talking about. And that night we had the task of raising money so that we could get some leaflets out.

I had one hundred dollars I had brought with me to start it off and to inspire women. This was the greatest evidence that we're serious. Not only were we willing to commit ourselves, but also we willing to commit our resources. And when I made the pitch that night, I said I'm starting off with one hundred dollars. There was a sister standing next to me, she said, well, I'm starting off with one thousand dollars. We made it a fun game, I said, you have really put me on. I only have one hundred dollars but I guarantee I'm going to get a $1000 to you. Well, that night we raised about thirty-two hundred dollars. And here we have $3,200 and that's the way we kicked off the women's contribution to the mayor. And we set our first meeting; we only wanted a few. Everybody had a responsibility to go out and multiply themselves. And we said to them, the only big shots in this women's contingency will be those who multiply themselves by a minimum of ten. Anybody who wants to be the leader can be the leader. Please just get somebody to follow you. That was a challenge. And we then set a meeting -- I don't remember the date, I think it was somewhere around February, the sixth, at Liberty Baptist Church. That was our first big rally. We were going to have it at Liberty Baptist Church. And the women went forth to multiply themselves.

But that night, there were women who were really put out with us because we didn't write them. I want to be a part. Well, you can be. Forgive us for not writing to you. But you now are a part. And everybody who wants to be. But don't leave anybody behind you. When you look behind, be sure you have somebody following you.

So that Sunday evening, we left church and we went to Liberty Baptist for the meeting. I thought I'd get there a little bit early so we could get things set up and we'd see how our tables and our mikes were functioning. We had our programs and things all arranged and our leaflets. And when my husband and I drove around, trying to find somewhere to part, it was 2:15 and the meeting was scheduled to start at 3:00 and you could see people coming, just flowing down the street. And cars were everywhere.

Well, I can't begin to tell you how my heart began to leap and how I began to just thank God for what was being made possible because we dared to believe and to reach out to each other. And we filled that place. I remember one of the articles in one of our daily newspapers was saying, for the first time we got a feeling that Harold Washington really had a campaign on. He visited us. Also he came and spoke that day for us. And we raised, in cash and commitments, over forty thousand dollars that day.

We had several rallies where women demonstrated their serious commitment to this campaign and to change. They never let us down. We had a marvelous team. And I dare say, we committed ourselves to fifty thousand dollars in that first campaign but we raised over one hundred thousand dollars, not to mention all of us were members of other groups.

The women raised money. But they also recruited votes; they got people out; they educated. They shared with their families, with their children. We served as speakers around this city and other parts of the country. They put on fund raisers in their homes. Some of them sold pies and so forth. We started off asking every woman to be responsible for at least raising one thousand dollars. You may not have it give, but raise it.

I can recall so vividly, I was attending the meeting at PUSH, one Saturday; our meeting was to be on the next day, on a Sunday. And I came off of the PUSH platform. There was an elderly woman who stopped me right by Reverend Barrow's office and she said, you don't know what this has done for me. She said, when you asked us to raise one thousand dollars I went home and I told my son that I was going to raise one thousand dollars for the Harold Washington campaign. she said, he yelled at me and said, "are you out of your mind"; you're on fixed income. Why would you make a commitment like that?" And she said, Rev. Wyatt, I sold pies, I sold cakes, I made sandwiches. And she said, I have right here with me now to give to you this twelve hundred dollars that I have raised. I said, honey, God bless you. don't give it to me. I don't collect other folk's money. But when we get ready tomorrow, at our rally, when we get ready to march with our contributions, I want you to lead that march.

Here was a senior person on fixed income who had sold pies; she marched that next day at our rally. We had the women to come down the aisle and we had barrels where they could drop their monies. Reverend Barrow oft times served as a person to make the announcements and to make the appeal. And as they came down and gave their checks, she would call their names off. And it was one of the most beautiful experiences which I have ever seen.

And at the conclusion of the campaign, there stood an elderly retired woman in a red wool dress, as beautiful as anyone you want to see. She said, honey, listen, what are we going to do following this. She said, you all have turned me on. I've never worked in any political campaign. She said, I'm turned on and I'm not going back. What are we going to do next? That was the spirit of those beautiful women.

Well, you see women are the majority in our churches. But those are the same women. That's why I say that we gave more than one hundred thousand dollars because we helped to raise monies in our churches. I'm a trade unionist and I have to raise money in the unions. Wherever people were, we worked. We took credit for what we did as a women's organization or Women for Washington, but that wasn't all that the women did. And you see in the church, we have always been included but not recognized to the extent that we should be.

We built our churches; we make them and we never really ask for our share of recognition. And then we have never challenged our male clergy. Because some of us feel that way. We never challenged ourselves to the word of God which calls us to be one.

The other thing is that unless I'm misreading, I hold that from the beginning God had set in motion what God intended. God created man and it was God who said it was not good for him to be alone.

And God did not create for him just a sex partner. God created a helpmate, somebody suitable with intelligence, with wisdom, with understanding; somebody who could have shared faith; someone who could make the two if not the three, where God would be in the midst of them.

I think they should be full partners. I've been married to my husband 48 years this year and usually in speaking and sharing with women who need the encouragement (and for men too) it is important to note that it is appropriate for males and females to function as co-partners. That's the way God made it that we should share in the partnership.

And God told not just "him" but "them" to be fruitful, multiply and to replenish; take charge. God told them to take charge and manage these affairs; that's what God told them and not just him.

We wouldn't have the conflict which we have, I believe, in the male-female relationships if we thought of ourselves as complementing each other. What I can do, let me do it. What you can do, do it. And let's bring it together for the whole of what we're doing. Now some of the men that we've worked with for years on many campaigns, in union organizing struggles and other things, they knew that the women could move. We just got off and did what we could do; we did what is commonly understood amongst women and then we relatedly shared with the men. We had to develop our women's political sensitivities so that when they shared with men they could feel comfortable even discussing the issues at hand. They could feel comfortable even raising money. When the men stood up and said we raised ten thousand, we could say we raised fifty thousand.

What did Harold Washington exemplify that made women so attracted to his campaign? He reached out to them. And he let them know that he needed them. That's one thing that's so important to women. They can do fantastic things, especially if it is known that they're needed. And he, in no uncertain terms, let them know that they were needed. He would come to our rallies, come to our meetings, to thank us and share with us. That encouraged us; it inspired us.

Those of us who were in leadership, sat down with Harold Washington and talked about a program that would interest women politically. We asked if he becomes the mayor, what is he going to do for women and for their families? Because most women are concerned about their families and whatever they do, they don't do it just for themselves, they do it for their families. Even sometimes at the expense of their own welfare. And so, we were able to help him develop a program of interest for the women. He committed himself to put more women in his administration. He fulfilled that. And we used the slogan, "Promises made will be promises kept." We were later able to say "Promises made were promises kept." And so, he had a program. The women had an agenda that they were interested in and they presented that agenda to him.

When I approach Harold Washington about what God told me, that he was to be the mayor, it gave me the kind of strength, courage and influence that I needed in order to help others to believe in what we were doing. Even when so many people were telling us it could not happen. Together we strongly felt that it could happen and that God would help us to do it. We just had to get busy doing the things that God inspired us to do. And I do mean that God inspired us to do every program that was meaningful toward getting Harold Washington elected. I was very pleased, as many others were, that we did what was unbeliever by many and that Harold Washington did not fail us. What we promised people he would do, he did that and even more. We were able to say over and over again, "Promises made, promises kept." We were able to take the demographics and just point out to people, look and see for yourself. Even in the midst of criticism, he always got criticism, most leaders do, we were able to tell the story because we were part of it, we believed it and we had faith in it.

Therefore, when just a few months ago, when God took him from us in the peak of his career, we had met with him that Sunday. I was the chairperson of the dinner honoring him, sponsored by the Committee to Defend the Bill of Rights. On this side of it, we now call it the last supper. We presented him with a proclamation that was most beautiful and as I got ready to introduce him, I felt inspired; he had stayed with us for about two hours, sitting at our table; we were laughing and talking. And my husband had sponsored two tables from our church and there we were all together in what finally ended up being the last supper with Harold. In introducing him, I told the people how wonderful it was to have our mayor relaxed and sharing with us for all this time this evening. And I said he works so hard and we are trying to help him accomplish the goal that we have set for him. I then said, Mr. Mayor, it is good for you to rest tonight. I think about the words of the late A. Phillip Randolph, when he said, "The struggle is never really won, it's continuous." I said, you'll never finish it either. But we must do what we can while we can. Now, it didn't strike me then, as you know, as it did after three days that he was gone forever.

THE BLACK CHURCH AND THE POLITICS OF LIBERATION AS REFLECTED IN THE HAROLD WASHINGTON STORY

George W. Walker

My involvement with Harold Washington's campaign began in 1982. While one day reading *The Sun Times,* I observed an ad taken out by 50 Black ministers for Jane Byrne. I became incensed with that and felt that Jane Byrne had betrayed the trust of the Black community. I felt that there should be a group of Black ministers supporting Harold Washington. If 50 could come out for Jane Byrne, I felt that 100 or more should come out for Harold Washington. At that time, I picked up my phone and called Rev. Jesse Cotton. Surprisingly, I discovered that he, along with some other ministers, had already begun thinking along the same thing. So we arranged a meeting. The meeting took place at his church, Institutional AME Church. A group of us initially set out to first of all discuss the premise from which we would organize our group. We had many mutual feelings as to what was happening in the greater Chicago community, in reference to the mayoral campaign. And, of course, we decided that we would give everything we had in support of Harold Washington. We began to mobilize our forces. One of the very first project we took on was to take out an ad and not only have this ad in *The Sun Times,* but to also have it in *The Defender, Sun Times,* and *Tribune.* We set out to get 500 preachers, calling ourselves Concerned Clergy for Harold Washington. We were successful in mobilizing a large group of ministers from all communions and denominations that we could find. We got signatures. We got them to sign on the line, and we adopted a position paper that accompanied the ad to the news media. I was very impressed with the enthusiasm that each of us seemed to have in reference to what we were doing. That got the Concerned Clergy for Washington moving.

I have been actively involved in civil rights throughout my ministry. I came to Chicago from Columbia, South Carolina. I was in South Carolina in the 1960s during the lunch counter sit-ins. I was involved with the movement throughout South Carolina, in Rockhill, South Carolina, Clement Junior College, Friendship Baptist College and so forth. I organized a group of social activists in South Carolina. My entire ministry has been somewhat geared around civil rights and freedom for all of our people. Wherever I have seen an opportunity to be involved in social activism, I have not hesitated to do so.

Needless to say, when I came to Chicago in 1972, I was disturbed with what I found on the political scene with the Daley regime. Daley, if you will, "used" the Black preacher in this town to "oil" his machine; and he had his machine operating very well. I was disgusted with what I saw with the involvement of the Black preachers in Daley's machine. I've been opposed to that. I saw in Washington's campaign an opportunity to be actively involved in the quest for social justice.

Because I feel that Harold Washington's campaign gave opportunity for the oppressed folk in this town to really speak out and to see that at last they had an opportunity to voice their dissent with what they have seen the machine do. I think this is what gave Washington's campaign the momentum, the fact that so many people saw an opportunity to just speak out through this medium, and they did. I sensed this in my congregation and felt that my congregation wanted its pastor involved in the movement. I made an effort to keep the movement constantly before the people. I shared my participation with my congregation and discovered that they were enthused that I was actively involved in this campaign.

The church has to involve itself with the whole person, every aspect of the person. There was a time when I felt that the church should speak only to the spiritual aspect of humanity -- meaning that which lent itself to the hereafter, if you will. We understand well that we have to live on this earth and we're going to live here until we die. Therefore, we have to prepare our parishioners to live and we have to be concerned about their total welfare, their whole life, all of their involvements. This includes the social, political, economical as well as the spiritual. So I have attempted to initiate that type of ministry here in this community, and have involved this particular church. This particular church has the reputation of being the open church of the community. Every interest group that wants to meet, they know to come here because our doors are open for them. We do that for that reason, so that we can address ourselves to the total life of the community and of humanity.

We have involved ourselves in voter registration because we felt that it was important that every eligible person should be registered, so that they could vote. This is a God-given right. It's a right that many people lost their lives for, and it's a matter of motivating people in the community. I have gone from door-to-door myself with teams we have organized out of this church, encouraging people to get registered so they could vote. Our church is a polling place; the 32rd precinct of the 19th ward meets here. So we have gone through the community and have tried to be very visible in encouraging people to exercise their right to register and vote.

I think we are going forward and I think that the movement is very much alive. Sometimes I think the people lead themselves. I think they get ahead of the leadership most of the time. Right now, the movement is alive and I think the people will eventually roll over the so-called leaders if they aren't careful. There is a spirit that's in the people which I have the assurance is going to continue to live. I've attended many rallies and I have noticed that spirit and it has inspired me.

The Washington campaign came to this church at least five times, prior to the 1983 election. There were several campaign rallies that we held here in our church. this church, again, was pretty much the meeting place here in the 18th ward. Each time we wanted to bring the mayor in for the purpose of raising funds and to mobilize the community in the 18th ward, we usually met here at our church. We did that. We opened our doors for the Washington campaign. Surely, this congregation was always uplifted by his presence. They were amazed even, with his presence, because the man was so open. He had such a great spirit. He was approachable. From him just seemed to exude a kind of genuine spirit that people saw. They saw in him their grandfather; they saw in him their father; they saw their brother; they saw their uncle. They saw a great human being in Harold Washington. People reached out for him, and he reached our for people. He loved people and he reached out to them at all times.

The Black church, it seems to me, is facing a critical time. It's a time when the people that we seek to serve look more to the church for leadership. They look to the church for answers to many of the complex problems that they are facing. I remember when Mr. Washington, the Sunday morning he spoke for us, talked about the role of the church in providing leadership for the kids. He talked about the family life and how we live in an age and time now where family life is all splintered, with the absence of fathers in the home, and how the men in the church will have to extend themselves to be fathers for the kids who are without fathers. He dealt with what the role of the minister in the community has to be. He has to be a very strong and visible person i the community, simply because people are looking to the church and to its ministry for leadership. I believe that's our day-to-day responsibility as ministers. I think of my own responsibility as being one of seeking out the lost who pass this church everyday, the homeless, the kids who are misguided and who need direction. I believe that it is my responsibility to reach out to the youth and to try to give them a sense of leadership and purpose for their lives. If they never come to church on Sunday mornings, the fact that I have visited them, whether it's on the parking lot or on the street, or on the playground of the school, if I have touched them in any way, I have been successful. And I hope it will create a spark within them to realize that their life must have meaning and purpose. I think that's the legacy that Washington left us, the fact that you've got to do something with your life. You have to make your life count. And I think he succeeded in igniting that spark in countless numbers of young people in this city. And not only in this city, but in the world. I was in Jackson, Mississippi the day the mayor was stricken with his heart attack. My secretary called the church in Jackson, Mississippi and when I received the message, I then announced it to the Bishop who was presiding over his conference. When he announced it, the impact that the announcement had on people in Mississippi was gratifying to me, to know that he had touched people all across this country. Immediately, that entire church went into prayer and mourning for the mayor. He was just a great spirit. He touched people everywhere. And certainly he was a friend of mine.

THE BLACK CHURCH AS AGENT OF SOCIAL CHANGE

THE HAROLD WASHINGTON STORY

Willie Barrow

I met Harold Washington when he was running for the State Representative office of the State of Illinois. I worked in his campaign. He was very serious, articulate and didn't tolerate any foolishness. I enjoyed working in his campaign. He was electable. And it wasn't hard getting him elected. After serving at the State Representative level he then decided to run for Senator. So I worked in the Senatorial campaign with Harold Washington.

I really began to know him after Dr. Martin Luther King, Jr. was assassinated. Harold Washington was very instrumental in gathering the community as he introduced the first bill to make Dr. King's birthday a holiday. He needed a lot of community support. He knew how to reach out to the community to get that kind of support. So he had a lot of courage at that time. He was very courageous. He was an organizer and he wasn't afraid to bite the bullet. So he got the bill passed. He was the major architect of the bill and became the first one to make Dr. King's birthday a State Holiday.

Then after that he decided to run for Congress. When he became a Congressman, I think that's when all of us realized just how articulate and informed he was about every area of this nation.

So he dared to be different. Then after he ran and won that. A critical issue that spearheaded the movement which eventuated in the election of Harold Washington as Mayor was the discontent over the education of our children. Several mothers were not satisfied with the fact that many children in the Chicago school district couldn't read or write. So they went to jail a couple of times. And, of course, people felt that PUSH should get them out. And finally Reverend Jackson called me one night and said "I just think we should go get Dorothy Tilman and the others out of jail." So we went and got them out. And that's when the movement began. A real movement in Chicago began with women going to jail, getting out of paddy wagons and being knocked against paddy wagons. Then we began to organize.

After that we started going to the Board of Education. We took hundred of people to the Board of Education with us. Finally Nancy Jefferson, on the west side, and Francies Davies took over the Board of Education seat. And, of course, the community rallied behind them and the momentum started. So one day Reverend Jackson was on the Sunday Morning Live show talking about the educational system, in terms of inequalities and injustices. There was also a lot of police brutality around that time. One man said, there is a way we can get around Mayor Jane Byrne and the many problems created by her administration. He pointed out that she was getting ready to have a fair, the Chicagofest. She was bringing in many tope flight musicians. He then said we should boycott it. And Reverend Jackson replied, "a great idea." The next evening, Jesse Jackson called me and asked me to call Reverend Clay Evans and Reverend Steve Thirston and invite them to a meeting to follow up on the idea of boycotting the Chicagofest. We had this meeting, and he said you know I think we need to start picketing the Chicagofest and we're going to hold a press conference. The next day we called all of the community leaders together. And some of the community leaders said,"there goes Jesse again calling in the community leaders." We had about 30 organizations present. We began to picket the Chicagofest. The picket lines got larger and the community got all upset about it.

Since Stevie Wonder was scheduled to perform at the Chicagofest we called and asked him not to come. And then the people called other leading singers to inform them that we were boycotting the Chicagofest. They decided not to come. Then Black people refused to go to the Chicagofest. Well, we broke the Chicagofest. We got the community up in a victorious mode and everybody was cooperating. After we had gotten that straight, we asked, "now what are we going to do?" The people said, "we need to translate this into a voting registration drive." And we didn't have Harold Washington in mind. "We are going to change the rules. We are going to the Board of Education." People got to be deputized and Reverend Jackson started his movement called "PUSH FOR EXCELLENCE," where you first deputize the principals. Then you deputize the preachers and let the preachers start signing up people in their churches. Then you go to the welfare department. We said let's go where the people are. We realized that people were not coming downtown to the Board of Elections and signing up. But since they can walk to their church, and schools, we decided to sign them up right there. So we began to protest, we got the rules changed. We deputized the principals; we deputized the preachers. We registered many people in the first two weeks. We registered about 5,000 people in two weeks. And in six weeks time we had registered about 150,000 people, more than any other time in the history of chicago. Then a fever broke out and we called it "Voter Fever." And one of our outstanding businessmen, Soft-Sheen, Ed Gardner, agreed to sponsor "Come Alive in 85." And then we asked who is going to run. They tried to get Reverend Jesse Jackson to run; they tried to get Judge Petick to run; they tried to get Tom Todd to run.

So then Lou Palmer put together a list of people. We said, we're going to let the people pole who they wanted. We started out with 25 candidates for poling. We said, the highest five candidates would be considered. So it ran in the paper for several weeks; Reverend Jackson and Harold Washington were on the list. Well, Reverend Jackson said he wouldn't run because he was interested in running for President. Then it seemed like we couldn't get anybody to run, but by now the process had become a movement. The voter fever had broken out. We had put all of these people on the roll without a candidate. This was the miracle that happened. So then after a while we only had two people we were trying to get to run, and one of them was Harold Washington. Well, we already had the people registered. Harold said, we had to have so much money in the bank. So we got businessmen to put this money in the bank. Then, we said, Harold we have all of that. Then he said, I don't think I'm going to run. We went to Harold by night and asked him to reconsider. Finally, he made the commitment to run. This is the first time that I have ever seen a people's movement draft a candidate. The people's movement drafted Harold Washington. When he consented to run we called all of the preachers together, and that's when the Black Church became essential. That's when the Black Church became the precinct captain.

Not only did the Black Church raise the money, but it also raised the consciousness and created workers. Jane Byrne had 11 million dollars and Harold Washington had less than 3 million dollars. But we had over 20 million dollars in human efforts. That's why I think the Black Church has always been the place where all politicians have come. The Black Church is where Black people reside. It is what we call the Base.

Just an ordinary man, a nameless face, called up and just gave that idea to Reverend Jackson to boycott the Chicagofest and that man, today we don't know his name. But he was the cause of Harold Washington becoming the Mayor. He is the cause of the movement today. Just as an ordinary woman like Rosie Park, a seamstress, started the movement in Montgomery, Alabama, an ordinary person started the movement in Chicago. God uses ordinary people to do extraordinary things.

So when he ran the second time for re-election, not only did we organize the Churches, the beauticians, barbers, artists, the CPAs, the educators, and so forth, but we had a fund raiser. I happened to serve on the Executive Committee and the Finance Committee. And I'm here to tell you that Black people gave money. Don't ever say Black people will not give to a campaign. They gave the money. White people didn't touch him at first. But it was the Asians that helped. The Asians and Black people gave money. They gave into the hundreds and thousands of dollars. I remember we raised 15 thousand dollars one night at the Hayes Center called "A Dollar in the Barrel for Harold."

Everybody felt that they contributed to his campaign. That's why when Harold died there has not been a funeral like his in Chicago.

REFLECTIONS ON HAROLD WASHINGTON AS A SYMBOL OF UNITY IN THE LIFE OF THE CHURCH AND THE BLACK COMMUNITY

Marvell Williams

The first time I came in contact with Harold Washington was when he was persuaded to run for the office of Mayor of the city of Chicago. During the early days of the campaign he made an appearance at The New Mount Moriah Baptist Church, where I serve as pastor. When he came to the church I was serving as host minister of The Westside Ministers Conference. At that time I was Vice President of the Conference and Charles Murray was President. When I listened to him speak to us I was firmly convinced that he was destined to become the next Mayor of Chicago. It became evident to all of us in attendance at the meeting that Harold Washington had the necessary fortitude and courage to become the next mayor.

Now, why did Harold Washington come to the black church to make an appearance? Well, he realized the power of the black church in the political process. Consequently, in order for him to become mayor he knew that he had to generate interest on the part of the membership of the black church at large. This was in keeping with his own tradition and nurture. Having been reared in the black church Harold Washington was quite aware of its value and significance in the black community.

Whereas there was some reluctance on the part of some clergy to get involved in the political process, I think most of us considered the Harold Washington candidacy to be integral to the ministry and mission of the black church. However, shortly after the campaign started those clergy that were reluctant became activated and involved. We realized that ministry has to concern itself with the whole person, including the social, spiritual and psychological dimensions. In this way our involvement with Harold Washington was perceived to be consistent with the legacy of the black church.

Harold Washington gave the clergy an excellent example of what ministry is all about. He represented quality leadership. He was a man of integrity. The principles that he embraced were noble and true. He stood for better housing, quality education, and social justice in every area of life. He dealt with the outcast, the poor and the forsaken. He loved and embraced everybody. Those that appeared to be insignificant, Harold Washington took the time to relate to them. He made no basic distinctions between people. He made all people feel accepted with a deep sense of dignity.

Harold Washington was a person of rare magnitude. And, in order to keep his legacy alive, all of us must get involved. We cannot afford to move backward. We must move forward. It is the responsibility of churches to take up where Harold Washington left off and move forward. He has increased our knowledge of the political process. Certainly, the City of Chicago is better because of Harold Washington. He has enabled the black community as well as other oppressed social groups to regain a sense of self esteem. I cannot over estimate the value of self esteem for oppressed persons. Harold Washington was indeed an excellent role model for all of us. Therefore, we must find creative ways of perpetuating such a great and noble tradition.

As individuals we must do our very best at all times. We need to do as Jesus said to the blind man. Namely, "We must work while it is day, for when night comes no man can work." This means that we must assume responsibility for our lives. We must cover all areas of life with quality of leadership. In doing this, of course, we must keep God at the center of our lives. Otherwise, we run the risk of serving ourselves, rather than becoming servants of God. Harold Washington help us to see that with God's help all things are possible. He kept God at the forefront of the movement. And, if we maintain such a perspective we will be able to succeed in the fight for justice and liberation. But this cannot happen unless we are willing to do our part. God will not do it for us. God will work with us. But God will not change our circumstance without our involvement and participation.

I am confident about the future. We cannot know the future; but we know who holds the future. If the oppressed communities remain unified I think the future will prove to be positive. Harold Washington was a symbol of unity and togetherness.

Charles Murray

The emergence of Harold Washington represented God's handy work in history. Prior to his emergence I had some difficulty with how black clergy tended to be disorganized in the city of Chicago. We were separated based on such things as professional preparation, economics, role functions, status, and so forth. When I was appointed President of the Westside Ministers Conference I made a concentrated effort to unify the clergy. I recognized the fact that clergy on the Southside and Westside of Chicago were not working together. I attempted to overcome this barrier. Harold Washington contributed to the overcoming of this barrier. He helped all of us to realized the need to come together around a common cause.

Because Harold Washington helped us to get involved in a common cause, black clergy became a major political force throughout the city of Chicago. Suddenly, we realized that old traditions that had previously kept us apart soon vanished. We became a unified people committed to a single cause. Harold Washington enabled many of us to work together on various committees in ways that we had never experienced before. I believed that he was so effective in this regard because God ordained him to be the Mayor of Chicago.

I have lived in the city of Chicago for forty eight years. This means that I have seen many mayors go and come. But I have never seen a mayor as dedicated as Harold Washington. He had a deep sense of spirituality. His mission was divinely inspired. He tried for the office of mayor earlier and failed, but he kept trying. This is a good model for us. The way might seem difficult at times but we must keep trying. Harold Washington's success, in this regard, represents the success of all of us.

Because of him we have learned to help each other more significantly. As this was his mission, it should now become the mission of all of us.

Willie L. Upshire

During the time that Harold Washington was running for the office of mayor I was serving as President of the ministers coalition. I worked very closely with Charles Murray. I have become acquainted with Harold Washington earlier when he was serving as state senator. However, I must admit that when Harold Washington launched his political campaign for the office of Mayor of Chicago, I hesitated to support his candidacy. I didn't hesitate because I had doubts about his qualifications. Nor did I have questions about his ability to govern the city of Chicago. But what I needed was more time to decide which of the several candidates I wanted to support. After persistent prayer and considerable reflection I decided, unquestionably, to support Harold Washington.

I needed more time because the other candidates were asking clergy to endorse their candidacy. Some approached me. But I made it clear that I had become an advocate of Harold Washington. Also, I needed more time because I was aware of how many people were cautious about the viability of Harold Washington because he was a black man. Some felt that problems of institutionalized racism would militate against his effectiveness. They thought that racism would work against his ability to govern the city. But in spite of this I became convinced that Harold Washington was the most viable candidate. Although I didn't have a close working relationship with Harold Washington, I worked consistently for both his election and re-election.

During the campaign I preached sermons related to how I felt Harold Washington represented a symbol of unity for all oppressed social groups. Harold Washington was indeed a powerful figure. He was a great role model for many young black men and women. For example, many who didn't believe that they could succeed in life, Harold Washington demonstrated the contrary. He proved to them that with hard work and persistence, it can be done. He enabled all of us to hold our heads up and say that it can be done. Many young people began to say, "We are not going to give up."

When the Mayor started out in his campaign some people said that he could not make it. But he showed them that it can be done. The thing that made Harold Washington so powerful was his Christian background. He believed in God. That is why he visited the black church constantly. He united people around the principles which are inherent in the Teachings of Jesus.

Clay Evans

I have always been impressed with Harold Washington. I perceived him to be very sincere and dedicated to the task of liberation and spiritual transformation. He brought together effectively both the social and spiritual dimensions of ministry. He was committed and sensitive to the needs of the people. He represented the kind of spirit that I can identify with. I think the church helped to make him the kind of person that he was. I think that persons who are connected with the church have an added dimension to their life. It helps them to be more effective in everything that they do. In the case of Harold Washington, it made him a great politician.

Harold Washington was aware of where the power base is in the black community. It is in the black church. People believe in the church and Harold knew this. He was keenly aware of this truth.

Within the context of the black church Harold Washington built a deep sense of warmth, mutuality and openness which had positive implications for the community. When he was alive I don't think any of us realized the magnitude of Harold's legacy. The only thing that we have to do now is to put into practice the high level of consciousness which Harold represented.

The significance of Harold Washington as a symbol of unity is to be found in his holistic approach to human liberation. This is why his political campaign was so appealing to the black clergy of Chicago. The black church has always been about the business of building a holistic ministry in the black community. We have to be unified both in theory and practice. Ministry has to be concerned with housing, education, economics, politics, culture, as well as the spiritual. Harold Washington integrated all these components into a unified whole. He challenged us to understand that the church must assume its responsibility of serving as a vanguard of liberation.

Now, the question which many are asking is whether Harold Washington could have succeeded without the support of the black church? I am confident that he could not have succeeded without the help and support of the black church. In the first instance, Harold Washington knew that the black preacher has the authority to speak for his/her people. The black community has invested this authority in the black preacher. Knowing this truth encouraged Harold Washington to make constant visits to the black church.

Harold Washington was aware of the fact that the same sun which shines on "The Gold Coast" in the city of Chicago also shines in "The Ghetto." Therefore, he made every attempt to relate to both communities. The fact that many whites didn't accept Harold isn't because he failed to make an attempt to relate to them. However, he was able to bring about a certain degree of unity throughout the city of Chicago in spite of constant resistance from several ethnic social groups. If Harold didn't have courage and determination, he would not have succeeded.

THE IMPORTANCE OF THE BLACK CHURCH AND COMMUNITY ORGANIZATION IN THE HAROLD WASHINGTON STORY

Al Sampson

Although Harold Washington ended up losing in 1977, when he first ran for mayor, I felt that it was important to act as a witness in that process because I saw the Harold Washington story as an extension of Martin King's beginning here in Chicago, with the whole question of housing, voter registration and political and economic empowerment. Then I would move into a serious of events that occurred after 1977. The creation of Cybark which ended up being run by Lou Palmer. The Black men at the round table, which was a group of business and professional men, with religious leaders, like myself, Gregory Ingram, and James Mack, who is a professor in the Department of Black History at Elmhurst College. At that moment in history we were arguing with Jane Byrne about a Black person becoming president of the Board of Education. The Black Men of the Round table sent a telegram to Jane Byrne, while she was in Israel, raising the question that we not only wanted more Black board members but we wanted to have a Black person to serve as President of the Board of Education.

She sent a message back to us that was unacceptable. It gave us a rallying cry. That was important because two ministers ended up being in contention for that position. One was the Reverend Dr.

Wilfred Reed, who at that time was pastoring St. Stevens A.M.E. church on the west side and Reverend Kenneth Smith, who was pastoring the Good Shepherd Congregational Church on the south side. Reverend Kenneth Smith is now president of Chicago Theological Seminary, Chicago, Illinois. It was at that moment that Bill Barry came out in the front pages of the *Chicago Tribune* and called me crazy. It was at that moment we challenged the right of Jane Byrne's choice to even be selected, because he really did not live in Chicago. He lived out in the suburbs. We had an opportunity to talk to his pastor and actually do the research and ground work that made it possible for him to be eliminated from the contention; and Kenneth Smith ended up being the first Black person to serve as president of the Board of Education. And that was important. One of the kids, a student in my church, showed me his diploma and on it was the signature of Kenneth Smith, president of the Board of Education.

That coupled with the ChicagoFest boycotts, I think created the ground work for us to move towards this whole question of the Harold Washington election. The week before Harold Washington announced a group of Black leaders from across the City met with him at Roberts Motel. We were convened by Lou Palmer, Raynolt Robinson and Georgia Palmer. Raynolt Robinson was at that time president of the Afro-American Patrolmen League, and he was going through trials and tribulations because it wasn't fashionable for Black officers to be in positions of power. And I remembered during his trials and tribulations that he was made to stand in the alley and guard it. So there was a whole humiliation through struggle for the Afro-American Patrolmen League. In convening that leadership meeting, we discussed several names for the mayoral election. Several names were mentioned. The bottom line is that we ended up with Harold Washington. But something else occurred in that meeting. We not only agreed on Harold Washington, but we also recognized the fact that the first time Carl Stokes ran for the office of Mayor of the City of Cleveland, Ohio, he lost. And part of the reason why he lost is that he didn't organized the Black preachers, nor the grass roots leaderships. The second time when we went in to Cleveland with Martin Luther King, Jr., we pulled together the Black Churches and we pulled together the Nationalists. There was a famous Nationalist in Cleveland at that time by the name of Armad Evans. He came from the Nationalist community. Both the preachers and the grass roots folks just weren't communicating. Therefore, we became the bridge of communication. When Armad Evans registered to vote, it meant that the nationalist organization decided to participate in helping in the voter registration process. This process resulted in getting Carl Stokes elected as Mayor of Cleveland, Ohio.

Based on what we learned in the Cleveland experiment, we attempted to integrate our leanings into the Chicago situation. This is why we created the Task Force for Black Political Empowerment. I served as treasurer of the organization and Bob Starks served as President. The organization consisted of over a hundred church and community based social groups. Some of the noted clergy participating in the organization were John Porter, John Parker, and Henry Hardy. We ended up inheriting the name of Mau-Mau.

When the mayoralty process started Richard Daley and Jane Byrne attempted to relate to the black community through the black church. There were several black preachers supporting the old political regime, which both Richard Daley and Jane Byrne represented. Because prior to Harold Washington the political process in Chicago really didn't take the black community seriously. Consequently, the type of politics that manifested itself was what I would refer to as plantation politics. Many black clergy were given donations for their congregations by the old political regime as a means of control. But they nor the members of their congregations were allowed to participate fully in decision making processes. Knowing this we challenged those clergy persons to consider the Harold Washington candidacy for mayor as a viable alternative. Many of them responded favorably to our challenge. A significant aspect of our challenge was an Ad which was placed in *The Chicago Defender Newspaper*, The Black Church is Not for Sale.

This started the deep involvement of the Black church in the Harold Washington campaign. At this point, many clergy were appointed to various committees related to the campaign. Our ministry of liberation involved itself in every aspect of the campaign, from voter registration to fund raising. Many black clergy persons and their members became deputy registrars. In some instances voter registration boards were created among social groups in certain churches. Traditional church Christians became community Christians. The people viewed themselves as participants in their own liberation.

When Martin Luther King, Jr. was alive the institutional church became a resource of social change. But when he died the institutional church left the community and went back into an experience of inwardness. It ceased to realize its outward dimension. The struggle for us was to get the church back into the community. So, the Harold Washington election became that golden opportunity for this to occur.

Black churches throughout the City of Chicago became mobilized. For example, in Fernwood United Methodist Church, where I presently served as pastor, a lady by the name of Evelyn Carrie registered approximately two thousand persons herself. Evelyn Carrie's commitment characterized the involvement of the Black church at large.

After the election of Harold Washington, I was appointed to several committees in his administration. Some of them included the transition team, task force on hunger, steering committee, finance committee and others. In this regard, I participated with others in taking several thousand persons out to O'Hare Air Port because black persons were not getting access to jobs. We created demonstrations which resulted in the acquisition of more jobs for the unemployed, which included Blacks, Hispanics, poor whites and others.

As a result of this effort the Harold Washington administration created THE FIRST SOURCE TASK FORCE, which is designed to identify jobs with unemployed persons. I served as co-chairperson of the committee. Presently, inside the city government there is an office entitled, THE FIRST SOURCE TASK FORCE, which continues to identify permanent jobs for unemployed persons.

I think in any movement it yields itself to both positive and negative things. The positive things about the Harold Washington movement is that people started reading the newspapers more; they participated on talk shows more; he unleashed a dynamic that interfaced with every segment of the community. The Harold Washington election brought people out of themselves into a dedication to the community. This carried over into his administration. Because he hired many minorities, including women. He opened up the government under the FREEDOM OF INFORMATION ACT. He participated in holding hearings on the community development block grant funds, whereas historically the political process functioned as closed system.

After the election, many Blacks went back home into an ease of comfort trusting Harold Washington to deliver for them. Unfortunately, they put too much faith in a person. I argue that we should also put faith in the principle and the process and not in the person. The death of Harold Washington became traumatic for the black community because they felt that they lost their savior. They felt that Harold Washington was one of their own persons. He was a product of the Chicago area. But, again, we can't afford to put too much faith in a person.

HAROLD WASHINGTON

A CALL TO ECONOMIC DEVELOPMENT

George Reddick

I met the late Mayor Harold Washington when he was a state legislator in 1968. We took a tour to publish the crisis and hunger in the United States, as part of the follow-through to the Poor People's Campaign which, of course, was an SCLC national project at the time of Dr. King's death. And Jesse Jackson led the tour, which consisted of 12 to 15 cities throughout the state of Illinois. And when we were in Springfield, Illinois, where we climaxed the tour on two different occasions, the one legislator who was extremely helpful to us was Harold Washington. He was then the vice chair of the executive committee for the democratic side and one of the most promising legislators -- white or black -- that we had. Harold Washington as a senator, some time later, was to be the person who prepared the first statement on state set asides and also secured the national holiday for Dr. King.

On this particular trip, we were fortunate to have him with us because we were protesting the removal of several hundred million dollars from the welfare budget. It was close to 240 to 300 million dollars. And the major force in that, in the removal of that was the governor and the house speaker at that time whose name was Smith.

Harold Washington took us to see the governor and Mr. Smith. His documentation and meticulous detailing of the inadequacy of welfare grants and the need for an larger appropriation of funds if, in fact, welfare recipients would have just the bare subsistence, was so effective that we were impressed with him from thence forth.

As a senator, he did some impressive things. He was one of the authors of the human rights act for the State of Illinois; he also assisted in instituting affirmative action legislation.

Here at PUSH (People United to Serve Humanity) he announced his campaign for the state Senate. He was running against a may named Taylor, who had been a staff director for Mayor Jane Byrne and had been one of the machine's main cogs. Harold Washington at the time began to exercise his protest and his own independence of the machine while in the state legislature. And so our relationship increased as he began to use the PUSH forum as a way of announcing his candidacy. And he was frequently pitted against machine candidates. He first ran for mayor in the late 70s. Although he lost the first time, he made an impressive candidate. Because he had made such a significant impression, it gave him an edge when the black leadership of the community sought a candidate for black mayor. The people immediately drafted Harold Washington as their candidate.

After the word had gotten around that he was the choice of the black leadership, I was fortunate enough to be the first one, on this particular forum, to announce him as the future mayor of the city of Chicago. Now I'm sure that persons said this in various smaller gatherings, but we announced him as the next mayor of the city of Chicago. And as a matter of fact, during the campaign there was just tremendous excitement in our black churches. I have never seen that much excitement in the churches, not even when the Metcalf situation came.

Part of the thing that really drew Harold away from the machine was the crisis that occurred when Ralph Metcalf, protesting the police brutality which had caused the death of a very prominent physician in our community, very prominent black physician who was holed up in the hole over the weekend and was found dead that Monday morning -- from exposure and police brutality. Metcalf took his preemptive strike against Daley at that time and Harold Washington was the first of his inner circle to make a break with him in this regard. And so in that regard, there was a break from Daley.

And, of course, as a result of that Mayor Daley offered another candidate for the office of Congress of the first congressional district, it was Irving Franz. Metcalf became a symbolic folk hero at that point, both by resurrecting the kind of tremendous achievements that he had accomplished in the Olympics in the late 30s and once again in the community. He made the speech here at Operation PUSH that it is never too late for a Negro to become black. And that the incidents that had occurred in that jail overnight and the police brutality and all that symbolized about racism in the city of Chicago had convinced him. And so he took that turn and he did it successfully because he defeated Franz resoundingly although Franz was tremendously competent, a very able man. He defeated him resoundingly just on the basis of that total thrust.

I think people found in Harold Washington a very articulate spokesman. He was a person who seemed to, in some sense, articulate our aspirations in every way. And I think it was the right time. For example, preliminary to that, a man had called on "Saturday Morning Live," WBMX and said, we were very, very upset with Jane Byrne for removing some blacks from the Board of Education, Michael Scott in the particular instance, and replaced the black with a white person; all blacks removed from the CHA board were replaced with whites. Jane Byrne had already removed Gene Barnes, as chairman of the Chicago Transit Authority; she eased him out. And just a number of things were occurring, and Jane Byrne was beginning to move on Ken Smith at the Board of Education.

So there was enough anger. It is said that Jane Byrne had calculated this as a means of getting a black candidate in the race to defeat that candidate; thereby removing any future black opposition. She miscalculated. She really miscalculated because that man called in on the phone and said, "I think we need to boycott the Snow Queen's festival." If we will boycott ChicagoFest, it will in some sense, lift the consciousness of our people. It will resurface the whole question of how they are being deprived; how they are being discriminated against, and violated." And he was right. And Lou Palmer and others galvanized people around the slogan "We shall see in '83," and that just moved on and on.

But in the churches you had ministers who had once been in the "enemy camp," that had been in the old machine camp. And I guess you understand this in this way -- and I think it's important to understand it. We were simply enacting one of the more tragic aspects of pluralism. But in reality, the socialization of immigrants had been through their churches. And as the Irish and German churches became more established, etc., they became the establishment as far as politics were concerned. And so they were, of course, lined up with Mayor Daley, whoever was in fact the leader for the group was going to provide the benefits, that's who you lined up with. That is a reality of pluralism here.

It is also a reality in the black community; we had so little voice and people were acting apart from us and simply exploiting us for their votes; they were giving us a few crumbs, public assistance and CHA housing in exchange for it. All of which did not constitute power. That fact, I think, was the anger. We had no power, we could not act or speak for ourselves. And the few blacks that had emerged were, by and large, functionaries; they were not powerful figures on their own. And here we had all this massive contingent of a vote that was going 88 to 95% for the democratic party, an absolutely dependable vote, it didn't make sense.

In effect, what people saw in Harold Washington was an opportunity for liberation. One old lady was to say upon his death and to put in one of the memorial statements that appeared, "He snatched the chains off of our minds. He made us recognize that we are ourselves capable of achieving. We had votes and we had ability." And that he proved, while he was downtown during a time when all forms of disruption were taking place, that we can achieve. He demonstrated his ability to lead. And that was evident even during the campaign; and it was in this kind of thrust, and their ministers emerging again with an initiative for a black mayor that looked like he could be a winner, that we began to see tremendous excitement in our churches. Our churches raised money for Harold; our church women were involved in the Women for Washington, and there's been nothing in the City of Chicago to match that phenomenon. The Women for Washington was almost something that rivaled the thing that A. Phillip Randolph was able to do in the '40s in several of our cities, in terms of galvanizing support.

I think what we saw here was a man able to galvanize support among our ministerial leadership and excite our churches. Those buttons were worn proudly. They represented, in some sense, what we Methodist say, a real "march to Zion." We were really excited about that. Churches had massive rallies for him. They were excited about his presence when he would come to the church. IT would just literally electrify people and everything. IT was just the right thing at the right time, and they had the right man to galvanize it in every respect. And we had very good leaders, very good leaders in the churches.

I think we need to go back to this point. One, as you get into office you recognize that there is much pain in maturity, particularly political maturity. When people found out that he could not wave a magic wand, there was disaffection you see. His attempts to bring the city all together were tremendously impressive, but were understood neither by blacks, in some instances, nor by many whites. Many whites admitted upon his death that in providing services for the city and the way he conducted himself as leader he was matchless. But during his life they could not see that, they could only see that when he died. There were a number of northwest side people that said, "he was my Mayor."

But what it says among other things is that there was pain; there are certain problems brought on by political maturity that are difficult to deal with. Now I guess, what I am saying is that we must deal with those things now. Our city is going through a veritable trauma over not just his death, but what was perceived as a manipulated process in which a mayor was placed in who was not the choice of the vast majority of those who were carrying Harold's legacy. Not it just so happens that the process was a process that was put in place in the place of having no process at a time when a roman conspiracy denied Wilson Frost the opportunity to be mayor although he had been council chairman pro tem. But that's almost another story now.

I think this is symptomatic and symbolic of what must take place throughout our nation, but especially in cities like this. We must work assiduously to prepare our people for the future. The thing that was impressive about Harold was, for example, he would go to Wall Street and people would comment about how well he knew his numbers. Therefore, he could sell the city's bonds. That's very critical. Many, many political leaders can't do that. And what it means for our kid is that they must take school seriously enough to know that one day you may be a mayor or a comptroller or a budget director like Sharon Gist Gilliam; this extremely gifted and fantastic women who is now chief of staff for the mayor. And you need to have ability because when you're dealing with 4 and 5 billion dollar budgets you can't guess in left field; you must come to terms with it. And to understand, for example, that massive cyclops of over 145 thousand people, the second largest city in Illinois, called CHA, management, assurance of services, effective policy review, a new direction for that constituency. That has to be a part of the agenda.

What I get frightened about is to have, for example, an example of what we saw just a few days ago. Our staff, our associate staff director, Jeanette Wilson, was talking about one of our student leaders who came to her, talking about they're discriminating against me, president of the Association of Black Students, but her average was 1.5 And while I know they discriminate against us, it's hard for me to absorb that 1.5 is totally the responsibility of racism. I can't go along with that. Some of us were in college 30 and 35 years ago when they didn't want us in school either.

And I guess what I'm saying is our students must take seriously what all these gains mean. 289 mayors, 6,454 black publicly elected officials, 3,340 in the south alone. What that means to us. We must take that. Our mayors are controlling budgets of nearly 40 billion dollars. What does that mean? We've got to begin understanding a billion dollars as translated into 16,000 to 18,000 manufacturing jobs and 45,000 jobs in medical fields, and 50,000 jobs in retail. We've got to understand what that means. And our kids are going to have to take over businesses, and they're going to have to establish businesses that can conduct and transact business with cities the size of Chicago. They will have to hire people and put food on folks' tables, because we are not going to see a day in which between the federal government and large foundry manufacturing centers, unemployment will be absorbed. That isn't going to happen any more. We are losing our manufacturing base. *Business Week* says that an average of 265,000 jobs are leaving us in manufacturing every month.

Now how do you, what do you do to restore the job base, not the manufacturing base, it's gone. That kind of thing, and industries like the auto industry where we have lost 450,000 jobs and about to loose 500,000 jobs more where 1 in every 9 auto firms, 1 in every 9 auto plants are expected to be closed over the duration. What do you do? And political education is essential to our community keeping its cohesion and voting intelligently. Understanding such offices as clerk of the court as having something to do with your life, when we are over 70% of the problem in the criminal justice system. Having some focus on what it means to have county offices as increasingly the county is called upon through its taxing powers to take up the slack that is present in the larger arena of government, etc. Having a decent public education system which means commitment on the part of parents first and then teachers and educators. But it is also, especially when kids come to accountability; it also means commitment on the part of those young people that we are going to have a good school; that we are going to perform in ways that will assure us accreditation, and not only accreditation, but will assure us that 90% of this class is going to college. And when we send a class in of 1500 students, we are going to graduate no less than 1200 to 1300 of them and not 250 to 400 of them. Like we do now. Forty-three percent dropout rate in states like Texas means 17.8 billion dollars in lost wages over the future 10 year period. We have got to come to understand that, in terms of our own situation in life.

State legislature races, how critically important they are, an dhow important it is for blacks to, in some sense, bargain for offices beyond that which offers them personal plums. The trouble with blacks is that in many instances, contrary to the accountability imposed upon white politicians, our guys go in there and do for themselves. We must understand that we have a commitment to our community to do for that community.

And then I think we can interpret it in this way. We need not interpret it as some kind of selfish ethnocentric focus. For when blacks are able to make their contribution, fewer of them will be in jail, and jail is $17,350 per cell per year as over against $3800 to $4200 dollars for high school per year. Fewer of them will be on welfare, which is now at AFDC $17.6 billion per year. That money can be translated into more productive industry on the part of us personally. Our incomes, if lifted to parity, that is if we are at $25,000 rather than $16,000 and $17,000 in median family income, etc. then we will be able to put more in the tax till, which will provide a greater basis for the kind of growth that we need and everything like that. And while we are a young race, we must learn to spend the $238 billion, or $24 billion dollars that are made in the city of Chicago, in our community. When we do, we will be able to bargain for better services from the other community.

HAROLD WASHINGTON

A CHAMPION OF HOPE

Sylvester Brinson, III

I worked with Harold Washington when he was a congressman. At that time I served as pastor of the Englewood United Methodist Church. O.D. Young who was a social activist in the Englewood community, knew Harold personally. And so upon becoming the pastor of that parish, I learned that frequently she would invite Harold Washington over for breakfast. And so she invited me to come and so that's how I got a chance to know him and sit down and talk with him over breakfast approximately once every four months. And when the community drafted him as a viable candidate for Mayor, we began to work with him much closer.

Our participation included assisting in putting together what we called a council of black churches. And I served on the executive committee as the chairperson of the nominating committee. Also I was a member of the Board of Directors. We pulled together the council of black churches in order to do some programming. But it evolved into a larger kind of mechanism once Harold was drafted. My role was to assist in coordinating programs and to coordinate the clergypersons meetings. In this capacity of helping to coordinate the meetings, I worked closely with Sampson, Cotton, Reed, Jarrett, Walker and others. We worked together as a team. And because I served as a co-convener of the minister's division of Operation PUSH for religious affairs, I spent much time coordinating meetings with clergypersons.

To talk about my role as a clergy within the community. I participated with Harold in a mass voter's registration. In fact, I became a deputy registrar and participated with Harold Washington in training over a hundred clergy persons to register persons to vote at a breakfast with him.

There are so many things that I think went into the campaign, from making sure persons were registered to vote to getting those back on the rolls whose registrations were challenged. From making sure that those who were poll watchers were relieved to making sure that they were fed.

Well, as I participated with Harold Washington I noted that he was a son of a Methodist minister, came out of the black church tradition. I was down at the center in the McCormick Inn and I saw grown men -- 65 years old and over crying -- it was a very moving experience for me to see the elders of the community, senior citizens actually crying -- whimpering like babies. I went over to see what was wrong. And they said, "Son, you don't know, we didn't think we would see it in our day. We had no idea that we would see this legacy happen in our day." Then I began to see that within the focus of the community structure itself, there was a need for the black church to really become involved. It seemed to me that the black church, in a sense, had lost some of its fervor, creativity, and its rightful footing within the community at large for black people. In the past, according to E. Franklin Frazier, the black church did some of everything for the black community. But as blacks moved north and became much more urbanized and assimilated, we lost our religious dimension. And I believe that if we can recreate that dimension as a people, the family ties will become better solidified. The black church is what we, as a people, own and control. If we can integrate politics and community development we would be able to alleviate crime, problems of the homeless, illiteracy among our children and joblessness in the community.

The community at large was in support of Harold Washington. And I noted that there was a spirituality of the community at large. And it seemed to me that the social activists were at the forefront.

However, a lot of people who were leading social activists, were not members of a local black church. It became clear to me that we cannot move toward a community of the whole without understanding the spiritual dimension that has brought us thus far. And so out of that concern, we need to organize community organizations containing a foundation in the black church tradition.

Harold Washington came to the churches. I followed him around -- because I also work in the political structure as a chief of staff of one of the alderman/committeeman, Allen Streeter of the 17th Ward.

An outreach ministry should do five things. It should seek to create, stimulate, provide, engage and implement action oriented programs. Once, we feel that we need to be about the business of creating a spiritual ethos by which people can begin to relate together harmoniously. We feel that one of the things, even with Harold Washington, which is needed is to gather diverse ethic groups together in unity. But I firmly believe that this did not develop for Harold Washington solely from a philosophical understanding; but it contained a spiritual undergirding. His spirituality possessed a quest for social justice. He grew up in the black church and the black community. When he joined Progress Community Church he began to talk about what it means to move from a spiritual standpoint. I think his spiritual approach enabled him to motivate people and bring them together. So I believe that if the community and all of the various ethnic groups will work together, it has to be done with an undergirding of spirituality.

Then it is essential to stimulate the faith community. I feel that the faith community needs a little stimulation. And that the faith community needs to understand there is an integration of the secular and the sacred. And our organization should unite with other groups around the premise that if we're going to really build the faith of our people, we need to deal with empowerment. To do this we must have workshop seminars, and training events dealing empowerment. There is a need for church and community based organizations to relate to the physical, mental and spiritual dimensions of empowerment. Harold Washington's administration related to each dimension quite seriously.

Then, we need to provide; after we've stimulated something, created possibilities and stimulated persons, then we want to provide for a nurturing, in the understanding and participation of the Christian experience. We feel that to be a Christian calls one to participate in the total meaning of the faith. The total essence of one has to be engaged when Christ enters ones life. So, therefore, church and community based organizations need to be able to nurture persons. Harold Washington encouraged such a process.

Where do we go from here? You know its not enough to bring people into the church and community based organizations. How do we nurture persons to grow in grace and knowledge? As Jesus increased in wisdom, he also increased in the spiritual and social dimensions of life. We need to give people time grow in grace and in knowledge in a nurturing process. So our Harold Washington put great emphasis on the nurturing process. The city council, to e warring to the 29 versus the 21, were manifestations of how Harold approached the nurturing process. He was steady, because he understood the value of the nurturing process. You're talking about a city that has been racist; a city that has been divided.

And out of his Christian experience, I would say Harold was a good example of what we try to do, that is how you bring people together and nurture, and give them a chance to grow.

And then to engage while one is growing. To engage in self-definitions for reasons of being -- why am I here? what is my calling? why do I exist? I mean, am I just born to be born? I think Harold knew the answer to these questions. People say that he didn't take care of himself. I say on the contrary, he gave his life for what he believed in. He was quite immersed in the political process. He was very immersed in the feelings of the people. Just as "Jesus was touched with the feelings of our infirmities," Harold Washington was touched with the infirmities of the community. The city of Chicago was his cross to bear. And, I believe that when we engage people to understand their reason for being then they can truly act out the commandment, "Love thy neighbor as thyself." But you can't love thy neighbor until you understand who you are. And when you define your reason for being and start moving towards self-actualization, you begin to love others. Upon tolerating your own deficiencies, you can better understand the needs of others. I think this is another thing Harold Washington was able to understand.

And then to act. I see our ministry, acting as a catalytic agency in the resourcing for the Christian community. There are a lot of brothers and sisters in the community that need networking and resourcing. We want to put together a talent bank of entrepreneurs, business persons, people of all walks of life that we can refer and direct resources in the community. As people discover who they are, they find out they're a part of a body ministry, a body community. How do you take people who are warring against each other? So we see ourselves as a catalytic agency.

Harold Washington was always into the fine arts. Before he died he was talking about building a new library where there would be teaching and training of young people and senior citizens to express their arts. They had an art show. You know ChicagoFest and all those others things; when ever you went to the ChicagoFest and other cultural events you had a sense of the arts and the gospel theatre and all kinds of things through the human resources division. Harold Washington legacy provided for the fine arts.

Well, as I look at Harold Washington, when he died the sermon the following Sunday was "The King is Dead, Now What" taken from the passage of the year when King Uzziah died, I saw the Lord. I think what we need to understand is that Harold was immersed in the quality of life and the betterment of all persons -- to move a city to what he said, "Chicago works." To give everybody a fair chance to say if you are qualified, you have a chance. And if you have not qualified yourself, we will provide a process by which you can become qualified. The challenge for me as a black preacher is to say to people, you must qualify for life. And our challenge as a ministry is to qualify you to qualify. That we want to engage ourselves on the cutting edge of where people are. Yes, they hurt but at the same time they must laugh. The pain is there, but there is hope. And that's why our organization is called hope. Because if faith is the substance of things hoped for, in order to get faith, in order to believe in something, you've got to hope to have something. So Harold left us a legacy of hope. To say, "Look at this, I leave you some things, I give you some substance. You can work together, I'll leave you some substance. You can train together, I'll leave you some substance. You can take powers that be and put them together and make a city.

BLACK EVANGELICALISM AND THE POLITICAL PROCESS AS REFLECTED IN THE HAROLD WASHINGTON STORY

Clarence Hilliard

I had a diverse role in the Harold Washington political campaign. I;m a member of the Baptist Ministers Conference. I also serve as secretary in the West Side Ministers Coalition; this coalition grew out of the Baptist Ministers Conference and became the action agency. This happened because the conference felt limited as far as it's ability to actively participate in political activities. We formed the coalition in order to avoid jeopardizing the standing of the conference. I have always been very active in the political process. In fact, when Senator Collins was running, I worked for her campaign and I became her campaign manager for a short period of time. I also serve as Chairman of the Board of the National Black Evangelical Association. And that group of ministers that move in a different circle. I tapped that group, I have served as their social action Chairman for a number of years. And I was able to mobilize that group in the campaign for Harold Washington.

The campaign for Harold Washington really got started when Danny Davies came to our west side group and shared with us the real possibility of the election of Harold Washington. Given the break down of black voters in the city and the fact that there were going to be two white opponents, we knew that if we could get a solid black vote, we could elect Harold Washington. This recognition kind of got to us. And while we were thinking about it a certain group of clergy came out in support of Jane Byrne. And others had planned on coming out for Richard Daley. This served as the pivotal event that aided in launching the Harold Washington campaign. So the Black ministers around the city pulled together and formed the ministers for Washington organization. We worked seriously in the campaign. The campaign began to gain momentum very quickly. A lot of people were saying it couldn't happen. They said Chicago wasn't ready for a Black mayor. And my question was always, "Well, why are you sending your kids to school if there is no future?" We decided to get started. The black Evangelicals organized and really got behind it. We got involved in the issues of the campaign. This came easy for us because black Evangelicals have always been very active in these sorts of things.

The Evangelicals of whom I represent had no difficulty with participation in this political process? Our hearts were thrilled and we just went full blast in the campaign. We raised money like everybody else, invited people over, held meetings, and so forth. We participated in the general meetings that were held on the west side of Chicago.

Why is it that Harold Washington was able to unite the south side, the west side, the north side and other components of the Black community that in the past have been rivals? Why is it that all of us came together? Well, one could raise the same question about what happened when Martin Luther King, Jr. came to Chicago.

A controversial issue facing the Mayor was the Gay Rights Movement. and a number of cities around the country have passed legislation that have a lot of our churches spending money in court fighting situations that they should never have to fight. Money that should be going for missionary missions and educations is going to fight Gay Rights issues. Now that movement started in Chicago under Mayor Byrne. The resistance of that movement was spearheaded by Reverend Crawford. And I don't know how he did it, but he rallied blacks and whites. Crawford is a unique man. We worked and fought this whole matter under Mayor Byrne; the West Side Ministers Conference just stood together on these issues and fought on them and prepared papers and resolutions on various kinds of things. Our position on that was that homosexuality is a sin worse than all other sins and we feel that, as God loves all that he loved them as well. Our problem was that when you enact legislation then you legitimize it. You make wrong right; and those people who oppose it, you make them wrong.

In 1983, when Harold Washington was running for mayor, we questioned him about the problem of Gay rights. And I said to Harold Washington that some of us need to get with you and talk with you, because Gays are pushing that whole thing. See that was a thing that they were really pushing. And we, the Ministers, wanted to meet with him and he said OK. We called and set up a meeting. We held it down at the Holiday Inn. The Mayor met with us and we laid out the issue. The West Side Ministers, and other ministers from all over the city were present. I guess we had about 75 or more ministers in that meeting. We laid out our issues and concerns. The Mayor came and shared with us his background and concerns; and like most Black politicians, he saw it as a civil rights issue. He saw the Gay as being a question of civil rights. That was the genesis of the Gay Rights Movement, connecting it to Civil Rights.

Now we knew his position. He was honest with us. Although he was not opposed to it, he promised us that he would not initiate anything or that he would not be up front on this issue. Now we got that, that's a promise we got from him. He promised that he would not do anything to initiate legislation in regard to Gay rights. That was satisfactory with us at that point. I mean that's all we could get from him. But we could live with that. If he's not up front pushing that and he will not initiate anything on that, we thought we could live with it.

I think one of the things that has always been in my heart and in my mind is that the Church of Jesus Christ, if it is what Christ set up, its a community development organization in a holistic sense. Its concern about the whole person and all you know and to be concerned about that. If that is what the church is and I am convinced that's biblically what it is, well the Lord said he didn't want me to preach good news to the poor, open the eyes of the blind now give deliverance to the captives and liberation for the oppressed. You know that's covering all of those various aspects of life. Political, social, physical; all that is covered in that and Jesus said it's the spirit of God that has anointed me to do all of this. I feel that Harold Washington, i his message tried to build a city that works for all people and he did his best. He did his best to make Chicago work for all people. He opened opportunities for all. Well, some people said, they were no better off when he got in to office; but the point is that they had opportunities. They could go anywhere they wanted to if they could qualify, if they could do a job, they could bit on it and they would get a hearing.

THE SIGNIFICANCE OF THE HAROLD WASHINGTON STORY FOR BLACK WOMEN IN MINISTRY

Brenda Little

In 1983, before I was pastoring Christian Baptist Church, and was involved in ministry at Second Baptist Church in Evanston, I took an active role in campaigning for Mayor Washington. Not only was I there when the night when he won the victory, but I was there during those times when we were having rallies at various churches. I was active in the clergy group that met frequently at PUSH. And during the first campaign, I got together with several women ministers in the city of Chicago, and we decided that since all of the other professional women were having various fundraisers for Harold Washington, that we did not want to be excluded. So, several of us formed a group called The Clergywomen for Harold Washington. We had no funds to begin with; just the fact that we loved Harold Washington, we were for the things he stood for and we wanted to see him as the Mayor of Chicago.

In a matter of three weeks, we got together an ecumenical worship service as a fundraiser. And Reverend Jeremiah Wright allowed us to use Trinity United Church of Christ, along with Reverend Barbara Allen. All of us came together for worship. Not only did we have a grant time that evening, but we raised almost $1,000 dollars in that one event for the campaign. We had several women that preached that evening and we closed it out with an old fashioned prayer meeting; praying for Harold Washington as our up and coming mayor.

Our spiritual life should be integrated into all that we do. I includes everything that we do in life. It's not a separate little entity over here that we save for Sunday morning. The church should have something to say about who's going to be in leadership positions and making decisions for our people. I know that Harold Washington was involved in the black church. he grew up in the black church. All of the things that he was campaigning for, I believed in personally.

I also believe ministers, called out ordained clergypersons, should take a stand on political and social issues. This should be done not only inside the walls of the church, but we should have a concern about what happens to our people outside the church walls and in their everyday life. And so that's why I made the conscious decision to take personal time and personal energy to not only say, "Oh, I wish Harold Washington would b our mayor." But to, indeed, get out there and take some steps our some actions to doing what I could do to get him elected.

When I think about Harold Washington, the man, I think just his personality seemed to motivate women to want to work to get him elected as mayor. And I say that because for many women he represented a strong black male image. A man that was not afraid to take a stand for what he believed was right. A man that could not be bought. A man that loved family, a man that showed character and strength. And then a man who was concerned about the rights of women. He was concerned about us as a sex being put into positions and being paid less, not being given positions because we were female. He demonstrated that in hiring women, we should not limit them to positions that are reserved just for women, but they should be placed in positions that required knowledge; positions where women can make important decisions, sit on boards, function as managers and organizers. And so he let us know, he would let us know by not only what he said, but by what he did, that he was concerned about us as women, and not just a sexual object for a male to look at and get pleasure out of, but as women who have something to offer to society.

Harold Washington, the man, had such character and dignity about him that I remember on an occasion when he came to the Westside VA to speak to the veterans for Veterans Day, I was the chaplain who was designated to do the invocation, and the benediction. And after the service was over with and people were lined up to get his autograph, and to just get a handshake or to have something to say to him, I waited my turn in line to get my autograph and get my handshake like the other people; and I had my clerical collar on at the time. And of course, he remembered I was the same person that had given the prayer. When I talked with him, he said to me before he signed the autograph, "Now if I had someone that looked like you preaching in my church every Sunday, I would make sure that I would make it to church!"

Now I suppose that some of my sisters that are on the far extreme of where I am with the feminism and so forth, might take that as a derogatory remark. And I thought nothing of that remark. In fact, I was honored and I took it in the spirit that it was given. In that when it came from Harold Washington it came in a warm and genuine spirit, not one that would try to deflate me or look at me in any other way than a women of God. So I say that about the man, Harold Washington. The message that moved women was that of his sense of justice for all people. His message was that I'm going to do all that I can do to see that women are given their fair share, and not just black women either, women of all different ethnic groups. So that's why I feel that Harold Washington was embraced by such a large number of women.

The other thing I would like to mention here is that although Harold Washington was not an ordained minister, he was keenly aware that in most of our church's women make up over 50% of our congregation. And women tend to share special talents in fundraising. We do that in the black church all the time. And it became almost for us like he is going to represent us as a leader. Just like the pastor in the black tradition represents the people as our leader, Harold Washington motivated us to want to really work hard to get together in putting all of our efforts toward achieving a single goal. The women teachers, ministers, and social workers all had our various groups. You know, it was almost set up like a black church. The teachers for Harold Washington, the social workers and the nurses for Harold Washington. I was in two groups; I was in the black nurses for Harold Washington and the clergywomen for Harold Washington -- just like in the church.

I would want to look again to where we started. The man and the message and the movement. I want to us that because of how I see my involvement, my being blessed to live in the era of Harold Washington and how that has effected my life and how I see myself moving on this journey. And I would like to conclude by saying that when I looked and I saw a black man that could achieve what Mayor Washington achieved in the city of Chicago, to be the first black mayor of the city, meant he was a pioneer because he paves the way for somebody else to be a black mayor one day. I looked at him and I saw a man that was so determined to do what he felt he was put here to do. He had a goal, he took the necessary steps to reach that goal, and he wasn't in it for what he could achieve materialistically; the society, what society would say: "You have arrived." He wasn't in it for that. But he was in it for the good of the people, and when I look at all of that, I see myself, number one, because in a sense, a very small sense, maybe not on a nationwide basis, or an international basis, I do see myself in some areas as a pioneer.

And he had the stamina, the faith, the guts, the inner strength to say there and hang in there and ont give it up because so many were against him. And so I'm saying that because it just gives me that extra push that I need. I don't want it to be as hard in the year 2100, 2000, 21st century. I don't want it to be as difficult for a 16 year old girl who gets a calling to preach the gospel and then have to put it behind her and forget, try to forget that she had the calling because the only encouragement she got was that Baptists don't believe in women preachers. I don't what that to have to happen to a 16 year old girl that's coming up in 1988. And so, some have asked me, "Why have you made it so hard for yourself when you could have gone another way?" And I say, "Because anything you pioneer in is not going to be easy. It was not easy being the first female to be a protestant chaplain at the Westside VA. That was not easy. It has not been easy staying in the Baptist church and remaining Baptist. It has not been easy to get refused to preach in Baptist churches, and if it hadn't been for the Methodists, I probably wouldn't have gotten too many chances to be in other churches.

And so what I'm saying in conclusion, it's like if God has called you to do a work, whether it's ordained ministry, whether it's leadership in the political realm, whether it's using your gifts and your skills to reach out and help your people, and in turn when you're helping your own ethnic group and people, you're helping others too then do it. Do it to the best of your ability. Do it with everything that you have to do it with. And I'm just going to end by saying that I know there were times when he would get so much flack from City Hall over votes and issues and he got shot down so much. The press even shot him down, he had so many political enemies, but I'm sure that when it really got to him, he could find comfort in the fact that there were some that were in his corner and were supporting him. And that one, the one source of strength and support was the black church.

That's why I never give up on the black church because the black church is going to be here. Nothing's going to happen to the black church because when we didn't have anybody to turn to, we knew who we <u>had</u> to turn to. And this past January, I lost my living grandparent -- my father's father. He lived to be 88, Baptist all of his life, but was the first one to support me when I told him I was going to be ordained. And when he died, he requested that I do his eulogy. He had been a member of the Mt. Olive Baptist Church for 50 years and over -- deacon, trustee. And he requested that I do his eulogy and he had to be buried out of St. Lukes CME because the pastor refused to let his granddaughter do his eulogy. That's why I'm saying what I'm saying. But you stay there and you stay in the struggle.

HAROLD WASHINGTON AS A ROLE MODEL FOR BLACK YOUTH

D. C. Coleman

Now, when I came to Chicago, Mayor Daley was the Mayor of Chicago. And his attitude seemed to be similar to that of a benevolent father who would give you what he thought would be good for you. And, before I came to Chicago, I had a negative image of it. I thought that all Blacks in Chicago shared this negative image. But when I got to Chicago I found that all Blacks didn't share this negative image. Some of them actively supported Mayor Daley. Now, I will never forget an article that was written in one of the papers by a writer stating that Black people in the City of Chicago were not ready for a Black mayor. And the reasons he said we were not ready were number 1 -- we were divided. He said that when the people of Bridge Street (that's the community from which Mayor Daley came) came to the polls, they were going to vote for one person. But Blacks were going to be all scattered. Secondly, Blacks were not registered. He covered the percentage of Blacks who were registered and he said that most of the whites over there on Bridge Street were registered. Thirdly, he said if it rains on the day of the election, it is going to cut the Black vote in half. If it rains of the day of election, the people over on Bridge Street are still going to vote. Now he wrote that as a big article. I cut that article out and I talked about it from my pulpit, about what the man said about us.

But, things change. When Mayor Daley died and Bilandic was selected to be the Mayor, many of the Blacks were irritated because Wilson Frost was the mayor pro tem and many of them thought that Wilson Frost should have been selected to be the mayor. But they ignored Wilson Frost and went over his head and selected Michael Bilandic to be the mayor which I think started a lot of furor in the Black community. Meanwhile, Ralph Metcalf, who had been one of the staunch democrats, was becoming more enlightened, and independent and he broke with the democratic machine over police brutality in the Black community.

When Michael Bilandic was selected, we even had one of the members of Bethel, who ran for mayor prior to that time that Harold Washington, Ellis Reed, but he ran for mayor also. I think he ran the same time that Harold Washington ran the first time for mayor. Well, Bilandic won. Bilandic was perceived by many in the community to be weak in terms of his leadership abilities -- although I think most of the Blacks were supporting him -- there was a growing number who were disenchanted with his leadership.

Jane Byrne came on the scene; people referred to her as the Snow Queen. And Bilandic made some mistakes in terms of the Black community. Consequently, Jane Byrne was elected the Mayor of the City of Chicago. And I suppose that if Jane Byrne had really done her job as she should as the mayor, and recognized Blacks in the community, then Harold Washington would not have run for Mayor of the City of Chicago. But the fact of the matter is that Jane Byrne did not take care of business in the Black community. She ignored many of the important functions that were symbolic; for example, the National Urban League had a meeting in Chicago and she did not attend, a National Fraternity held a meeting in Chicago in which Mayor Bradley of Los Angeles was in attendance, but Jane Byrne failed to attend. There were many major functions which she should have attended, but did not. Secondly, in her appointments to the school board, she appointed whites to positions that were previously held by Blacks. This irritated many people. And I think it was the cause of Lou Palmer's coining the phrase "We shall see in '83." Also, appointments which she made in the CTA and the CHA aroused the fury of the Black community.

So that Harold Washington, who I think was perceptive in all this, had a great interest in the Black community. And I think because he had a history of being independent, he was able to bring together the various components of the city that other Black leaders were not able to do.

What made Harold Washington unique? I think is was his relationship with the Black church. Now, Harold Washington's father was a minister. His father served as assistant minister of Bethel AME Church. Each time Harold Washington came to Bethel Church, and he came there on numerous occasions, he always talked about his father being assistant minister. He went around with his father to speaking engagements and listened to him speak. And I think his relationship with the Black church enabled him to communicate with the people in a way that was just marvelous. He could come into a church and sound like a preacher. In fact, I told him we were going to give a license. His ability to communicate with people was unique. And people just rallied behind him because of that ability. So, Harold Washington evolved, from a member of the established democratic party to an independent candidate, and finally to one who was willing to do battle with the establishment.

I think there were a number of things that occurred as a result of Harold Washington becoming the Mayor of the City of Chicago. First, it raised the thinking of Blacks and especially Black youth, in terms of the height to which they could aspire and the heights they could attain. They no longer felt that there was a ceiling on where they could go and what they could do. It was very inspiring. Secondly, it enlarged the thinking of many wyo came to understand that when we think of social change taking place in the City of Chicago, they had to think of more than their particular self-interest. I mean we had to begin thinking about various social groups. He helped us move away from individual concerns to the concerns of the movement. Thirdly, many more people became involved in city government as a result of Harold Washington. It was just a pleasure to walk down through city hall and see the young

Blacks in positions of authority and in positions which they had not held before. And I did walk down through city hall on numerous occasions to witness this drastic change. For example, he appointed a Black superintendent of police. Blacks had been seeking for that position for a long time, but had been continually passed over for it. Harold Washington made the difference. Now of course we had a number of Blacks who were in positions already, but I think Harold Washington maintained them and also enlarged upon the number who were there. We already had a black superintendent of schools. We had a Black as head of the Department of Human Services; he maintained them. He was opening up new positions in the public library and the Chicago Housing Authority. He was working to change the Park District, which historically has been very prejudiced and segregated. He was putting blacks and other ethnic minority people on boards. I think his ability to do that in the Black community as well as the Hispanic community brought about a great change in the community at large.

I think also, as a result of Harold Washington being elected mayor, Blacks have gotten a lot of things that they didn't get before such as more participation in the legal profession, insurance industry, consulting services and contractual services. These things historically were closed to us, but they have been opened up to us, as a result of Harold Washington. He helped in getting funds placed in Black banks.

I have many recollections of Harold Washington and his visits to Bethel Church. I can recall sitting beside him in the pulpit. He asked me questions about the ministry and mission of the church. He was very interested in the church and its involvement in the community. I recall Harold saying that he was going to get us to license him to preach. And, of course, we did give him many certificates of appreciation.

HAROLD WASHINGTON DEMONSTRATED THAT "IT CAN BE DONE"

Henry Hardy

I think the Harold Washington election was essentially a movement; it was a crusade. Harold Washington's election keynoted a significant change in the American political experience and also the interaction of the Black church and the political process. Because it enabled Black ministers and churches to impact in a direct manner by creating political change which before had not occurred. It was an overcoming and a dismantling, to a great extent, of what we knew in a very negative sense as a plantation system. Prior to Harold Washington's election, Chicago was governed by plantation politics. But now we saw a legitimate people's movement, and that is why it was a crusade. It represented a surging tide of self-esteem and pride. It was a heightening of the human spirit, where people walked out of the darkness into the light of a new consciousness. And so Harold Washington became a symbol in the theological sense. He embodied noble values. He pointed beyond himself to the deep realities of the Black experience. And so when you looked at Harold Washington, in a deep sense, it really was an experience of self-transcendence. The movement transcended Harold Washington. Harold Washington at that moment in history, happened to be the vehicle or the vessel, in which this energy, this vision was poured. But I think at this point, the experience represented an integration of the man - the message - the movement. It was what the theologian Paul Tillich refers to as the **kairos**, meaning qualitative time or the fullness of time. And it was in that fullness of time that things came to pass. So I think that the Black Church was there in a very seminal moment in history. And when Black preachers spoke for Harold Washington, they were speaking not only for Harold Washington, but for the total Black experience. That gave the movement great dynamism. It was the type of dynamism that one cannot manufacture in a laboratory. It came out of the chemistry of the Black religious experience. People were saying, we're tired of living in the outhouse; we now want to move to the castle. And so it was as if all of the funding resources of the Black church came together at this pregnant moment in history and gave birth to a new idea. All of the hopes and aspirations of our foreparents became manifested in this movement. It enabled Black ministers, many who did not talk to each other, who did not have any prior intimate association, to come together around this common issue.

It was in the most sublime sense a movement in ecumenicity. We cut across denominational lines, as ministers interacted with each other. Some had earned academic degrees. And many had no academic degrees. The movement brought together persons from all walks of life. But it was a common sharing, it was a family affair in the election of Harold Washington. So I think that what it enables the Black preacher to do was to have a prominent role in the political process. It enabled the preacher t have an extraordinary impact in the community in terms of moving beyond a kind of pie-in-the-sky promise of future rewards. But here leaders were actively engaged in affecting systemic change, and I think that could not avoid enhancing the posture of the clergy. And that is extremely crucial. I think further that Harold Washington's election called us to a sense of our particular spirituality in the sense that we could recognize our true identity. The movement was the power of an idea whose time had come.

Of course, Lou Palmer's noted phrase was "We shall see in '83." And so it was from that kind of potency that we began to move. The Black Churches became the locus of much of the registration movement. I had persons in my church that participated in registering voters. Many Black preachers participated in the registration process. Churches were opened up to enable persons to stage an area for registration on election day. Churches here were stations for people as campaign and electorial stations. And many of us had polling places; it became a real participatory involvement on the part of the Black church.

It is consistent with the historical experience of Black people. The Black church has always been that motivating thrust; the vital dynamic element that galvanized and energized the vision of its people. Historically, the Black church has been the vanguard of the freedom movement. Dr. King, of course, in all of his activism in the movement always went to the Black church. So I think that the Black church, in a sense that one institution, which is unique to the Black experience. It is free and in that regard, it is that which captures the imagination of its constituents. It moved on to make Harold Washington's election a watershed mark in the American political experience.

I think we must continue to talk about what role Harold Washington played in terms of heightening the self-esteem of Black people. We must understand that we have been brutalized in our psyche. There has been a physic assault on the Black community. There has been a depersonalization of our being. And we have not been able to really stand up. And so I think Harold Washington's election signaled the fact that no longer would we ever be bought again. No longer is anything beyond the pale of realization. Now it is no accident that Jesse Jackson is running for the presidency of the United States. We are beginning to break new ground. It gives hope, aspiration and inspiration to young people to be able to say "Yes, we can." Harold Washington epidemized the spirit of "Yes, I can." They said it couldn't be done, but Harold said, "Yes, I can." Like the little engine moving up the hill, "No you can't, no you can't, but I think I can, I think I can, I think I can." When it got to the top and looked down it said, "I knew I could, I knew I could." It was in that context now that we talked about the dignity and triumph of the human spirit. So in that regard, I think there has been an awareness now that the Black church can rediscover its role and ministry. We don't just deal with the person as soul or psyche, but we deal with the person, in terms of the spiritual and social realities. And I think that becomes a broadening and maturing of the ministry. We viewed ourselves for the first time in Chicago as having some connection with City Hall.

Chicago, of all cities, is the most political reality. If you don't believe this try to get a building permit or see when you do things in previous administrations if you did things that didn't meet with favor if the building code inspectors or fire inspectors suddenly did not find all kinds of aggrevious violations. So I think that now we are beginning to see the church bring about social change. It is beginning to move out and make its impact felt in our total community.

HAROLD WASHINGTON AND THE VALUE OF CHURCH AND COMMUNITY DEVELOPMENT

Carroll Felton, Jr.

I first knew Harold Washington as a congressman from this area and had the occasion to meet and talk with him because he lived in the same building with my brother, Gilbert, who at the time was one of the assistant secretaries of commerce in charge of the census and population analysis. So we had an opportunity to run into each other and talk because Gilbert was close to him, even now, as he is with the congressman from this area now who is there in the same building in Washington.

It was during those days that I was fascinated by his visits. I used to visit with some of the black congressmen, because at the time I was the Director of the Urban Training Center for Christian Mission. I was in charge of the fellowship program, and later I served as Director of the Black Ministers' Project. My responsibilities included staying in touch with Black congressmen, or rather that whole black caucus group.

So I had an opportunity to work with Harold Washington early in his political career. I was always fascinated with his extensive vocabulary. He was able to understand bills and summarize them in one or two sentences. Those of us that visited the committee meetings would sort of punch one another and say, "Get them, Harold."

After the Urban Training Center experience, I left to go to Pittsburgh and lost contact -- well, not lost contact, I saw him in Washington -- but was not part of the first push for him to become mayor. Harold's ties within the Black church was a fascinating thing. Although we did have several congresspersons who were with the church. We had a strong person in the way of Shirley Chisholm and others. You could always tell that Harold Washington was part of the church. This didn't mean that he went around with a halo nor his hands folded; it means that he understood the significance of the Black church as an agent of social change. My argument is that the Christian church in general tends to put more emphasis on analysis than social action. The church engages in more social research than social reconstruction. However, since its inception, the Black church has been involved in the political process. An integration of religion and politics was part of the emphasis and influence of Harold Washington. It isn't that he used the church to advance his political career, but he was involved in the church to understand the process and attempted to enable people to overcome oppression. So for this reason, I certainly believed that Harold Washington understood that the Black church and the political process are inseparable.

But being a member of the Black church, he knew what it meant to believe the principle that the locus of one's life in the world has no limitations on the person when freedom is affirmed. Because freedom enables a person to choose the area in which he/she wants to participate.

Now, I believe that Harold Washington could make the choice even in the midst of what was a limited freedom for him, in terms of the environment. But beyond that, there was something within him that would always come out and basically in his humor. The few times that I talked with him as congressman, he would always say something humorous about the preachers. I never perceived that as being a put down. This sense of freedom helped him to appreciate the commonality of all persons. No matter who they were, Harold Washington could understand people in terms of their suffering. And the Black church helped to know the value of identifying with the oppressed. Also it taught him the fact that one doesn't have to become totally a part of a particular group in order to identify with it. And most of us know that whatever group that he could influence to think like he thought, in terms of the political process, he was able to identify with. NO matter whether there were negative forces rising to surface, he would be identified with them. Here again, the theological presupposition that seemed to undergird all of that was to understand folk; you don't have to be a member of the club in order to identify. But somehow you have to let the essence of your own being be a part of that to which you identify.

He was always positive with folk, even in the midst of the contradictions out in the world that seemed to hit him; in moments he would reflect upon a kind of humor. He would engage in deep reflective silence. If you were in a meeting with him and he said nothing for a while, then all of a sudden a smile would come on him. He would then have something to say that would just wipe you out. And I still say that this goes back to his early training in the church. The Black church gave to him an understanding of controversy, pain and suffering.

And I think a man like Harold Washington, with his understanding of the church, could say just enough to run us back to our pulpits to reconstruct our sermons. The Black church itself has given this kind of leadership both social and religious dimensions.

Many white churches that wanted to move into the political process, discovered that they did not have the freedom that the Black church had. They had to go through certain boards and things of that sort in order to get the okay. The minister in the white church became an administrator and the minister of the Black church became the prophet and priest. And the Black preacher never had to be told which hat to wear; he or she would make the decision on the basis of the particular situation.

Therefore, in the midst of a well-planned sermon, he could feel the presence of God to make a prophetic or priestly declaration. This has to do with the power of the Black preacher in particular and the power of the Black church generally.

The power in the Black church, then, to raise the level of its people, had no ceiling. There was nothing to prevent the people from going to where they wanted to go. And the reason there was no ceiling is because we were so far in the basement. And being that low, we could only look to the top. And we understood, with a deep sense of commitment that although the Bible talks about the ladder descending down to Jacob, we could interpret its meaning, without committing hermeneutical suicide, and talk about climbing Jacob's ladder. This was an impetus for us to move on a new level of freedom and understanding. Simply said, then, the empowerment of the Black church came from the folk, through the spirit of God. The strength was not only in the gathering on Sunday morning, but it was looking around and knowing that the neighbors who were suffering as you were suffering and who were as poor as you were poor, could somehow put on their Sunday best, walk into church, and snake loose the chains of poverty and oppression. And for that moment, to become free.

I remember writing that I had been taught that the shouting in the Black church was not in keeping with good religious practices, and that it indicated some need of psychological care on the part of the membership. And I was beginning to believe that until I saw the faces and talked to the folk who shouted, who stood up, waved their hands, saying amen. They had a new look. And I discovered that it was a catharsis at one level, they could take it all off and put on the new clothing of the righteous. Harold Washington understood that in the political life. His speeches were not dry; they were not academic presentations in the old sense. Even though he had a huge vocabulary, and that he could use words that somehow we had never heard. Someone used to joke and say, "Harold has created a new word!" But in the midst of all that, there was that inspiration along with the academic presentation, that made his speeches -- for both white and black -- sort of political sermons of what can be done when the new order comes. And in the language of the Black preachers, he could always relate the new Chicago to the new Heaven and the new earth. He was a political prophet, if there's such a one. But he was a prophet of our times who understood the basic things of the Black church that he took over into other groups without being ashamed. Those of us who heard him, would go and stand somewhere near him when he spoke to groups that had a majority of whites, waiting for that moment when he would do his white speech, and we discovered that Harold Washington had no white speech, no black speech, no blue speech. Harold had a speech that touched the hearts and minds of both; and in the midst of being challenged by eyes or some words, he could laugh.

I came up in a church in Washington, D.C., where I had a pastor who was the president of the NAACP. This was during the early days of World War II. I was just a little kid then. But what had happened, and I did not know that this did not happen in other churches, when people joined the John Wesley Church they had to join the NAACP that Sunday morning with their $2 membership. I did not know that this did not go on in all the other churches; so I subsequently became the president of the youth council of the NAACP in Washington, D.C. I had the opportunity to meet the early people like Walter White because he was in and out of Washington. So my understanding of the church has always been a church of freedom. A church that fights for freedom against oppression. Stephen Gill Spottswood was my mentor at that time. My other mentor was my own father, who, himself did not appreciate the ministry, because he equated it with poverty; so he went on to make money, but he decided that the rest of us would not go into the ministry. I went against his wishes but he later enjoyed it. And then I was put in contact with my mentor, Howard Thurman, and was under him for 16 hours of Philosophy at Howard University trying my best to understand what he was saying in relation to what was going on out there in the world.

For those of us who were mesmerized in the chapel on Sunday morning by this giant of a speaker, who never seemed to answer the questions that were politically astute for him and us, had some feeling that he did not complete the cycle. And then as we listened to him, he was at that point involving us in a world situation. His philosophical lectures in class were tailored at the point that we could move in any direction theologically or psychologically we chose to do that on. This was a rich experience for me.

But there came a time when I looked at the ministry and thought that it was not what I wanted to do and approached Dr. Thurman on the campus of Howard University to tell him that I was leaving. And he said that at the moment you become a professional preacher, you stop being a minister. He told me that it was a vocation. A vocation and not a profession. Well, what am I going to school for? I raised the question, if it were not a profession? And as be began to talk for about an hour and a half, I looked around and there were almost 200 students who had gathered without Dr. Thurman or myself realizing that a crowd had been drawn. Because he was in the midst of preaching -- right there on the campus of Howard University; between Stephen Gill Spottswood and Howard Thurman -- then I began to have some synthesis, some understanding. Because I was an activist from Dr. Spottswood's point of view and after attending the Quaker meetings with Dr. Thurman, I didn't know who I was. But it began to come together based on the influence of those men along with the giant Mordecai Johnson, who was the President of Howard University at that time and who preached at least once a month in the chapel while we were there. These are my early experience that drew me into an understanding of what it's all about. The pausing from and withdrawing from people at times that I had to do in order to get myself together. The preparation of sermons which changed for me in terms of being inclusive, trying to understand Dr. Thurman's use of the term "the for instance Jesus." And I began to probe to understand whether or not he really believed in this Jesus; he was saying that Jesus Christ was our for instance, for example. And that we could walk in his footsteps and when that illuminated in my own being, I understood who I was from that moment nd had no real problem since then in my articulation of the faith and being a part of the movement.

Subsequently, I became involved not only in the activities of the community, but I was involved in the sit-down strikes that were later called sin-ins. My first sit-down strike was with Mary Church Terrell of the late attorney Charles Terrell for whom the law school was named. And we went to downtown Washington, D.C. where everything was segregated and sat down there to have our first arrest. I went back to church to report to the congregation as part of the morning sermon that I was allowed to share with the president of the NAACP, who was also pastor of that 5,000 member church. It wasn't long before I went to seminary to try to understand what all this I was reading and hearing was about. I discovered that in the seminary that the president told us that if we had religion, it was fine, because we would not get any at the seminary. He said that the seminary would make scholars out of us and if we had religion, we could carry through. It was then I understood that the academic process had to be along with that desire within one's soul to do right. But one had to know what to do.

It was then that the NAACP in the city where I had been transferred as a Methodist preacher, Knoxville, Tennessee, was on the verge of being outlawed -- it wasn't done like Alabama, but it was during those days that the last Martin Luther King, Jr. put out a call to the presidents of the NAACP chairpersons, as I was a president then, to meet in the formation of a group called the Southern Christian Leadership Conference. I was not able to make that meeting, but I did attend subsequent meetings and moved into Atlanta to participate with Dr. King with 14 of my own arrests with this giant of civil rights.

The Urban Training Center for Christian Missions had been organized through 23 white denominations to train white pastors to deal with the civil rights movement in terms of being supportive. It was classified first as anti-seminary because the things folk were learning there were not being taught in the seminary. Dr. King discovered that this sort of training should be given to black ministers and along with the Reverend Andy Young who's now the mayor of Atlanta, Dr. King approached the national board of the Urban Training Center in order to have a fellowship for Black clergy who did not have the money to attend. And the Ford Foundation created a grant that was administered under the Reverend C. T. Vivian to give scholarships to Black preachers along with the Reverend Archie Hargraves who was on the faculty and staff of the Urban Training Center.

I went through the course, twice. And then when I went back to my church in North Carolina, I was called to become part of the training faculty of the Urban Training Center and subsequently was made its director in dealing with more than 5,000 Black pastors who trained at the Urban Training Center for Christian Missions on a very tight schedule. It was through this that I began to understand clearly the Black church's role beyond that which they had done. It was then that I began to se the Black church moving with a decided effort into the political process. It was there I began to understand housing as ministry. We could understand how to expand our churches into educational units, moving into day care centers. Understanding that we had to be in contact with our state representatives as well as our federal representatives in Washington. It was there that we learned how to lobby as Christian pastors at state government and on the national level. It was then that we began to talk about some of the leaders within the Black church moving into the political realm to be able to represent us with votes in those areas. Subsequently the black caucus was formed and with the Black congressmen in Gary, Indiana when Mayor Hatcher was elected as mayor, they called on members of the Urban Training Center to come to Gary with him to help put that government together. Subsequently, we went down to Nassua with the new Black Prime Minister, Pendleton, to help him in looking at what his government should be under the leadership of a Black person.

So the Black church, for me, has been the point of ultimate referral that has somehow brought light to the dark pathways through which we were groping. It gave me, and it is still giving me, that incentive to go forward.

After when there seemed to be a leveling off, and my inability to complete my work for the doctorate because of money and having to pastor, received a call from the Ervin Miller Sweeney Fund saying that I'd been selected to do the doctorate with 19 other persons in the Martin Luther King Fellowship, after years of struggling. And I discovered that of 20 selected, some of the finest men in the country along with Wyatt T. Walker and William Jones, Jim Forbes, and others in that group -- for three years we worked together. And here again, inspired to understand that the Black church is now focusing on another group that is left! Those young men and women who have gone to college and gone into business, and felt that because they were in the corporate world, they had to move to the white churches and the white communities -- hob nob and play golf. Nothing wrong with that but they miss the basic spiritual uplifting that they'd come back to in a crisis. And then back to where they were after the crisis was resolved. We are discovering now, they're coming back to the church and they're sharing with the church their skills in the corporate world and at the same time being part of the Black church that gave them their first opportunity to become leaders in the community.

So this brings us back to Harold Washington for the uniqueness of Harold Washington was that he did not have to make that jump into that world, even though he was a congressman, everything was open to him, he had sort of access to all of the corporate level being a congressman. But he remained in the Black church, for he knew somehow, that the basic structure of the Black church gave him his spiritual foundation would continue to be with him so the crisis level of his life was always lessened because he didn't have to skip it.

It appears to me in the context of relating Harold Washington to the Black church and understanding his political career, and his determination to do the thing that was in his heart and mind that had developed in his association with people, we do understand that Harold Washington had many choices. And I think we need to understand that even though there was a driving force to work with his people, he could have made other choices to do that. But the City of Chicago still fascinates him, because he always said, if you recall, he tried to even it on the occasion of his election. So it brings me to understand, it leads me to understand that through all of the experiences of his life were included into his whole self and was part of his whole identity, that the basic foundation of the Black church, though not spoken of, all of the time in terms of identifying it, but the identification came as a result of how he acted, initiated, and began to move in his political life. And even though at times he would describe Chicago ad the new heaven and the new earth, he also understood that there were times that he was a John alone on island of Patmos and he had to reflect upon life as a member of the Black church which gave him the impetus to work for the City of Chicago.

EULOGY OF MAYOR HAROLD WASHINGTON

B. Herbert Martin

Mayor Washington was not just a good mayor. He was great. He was faithful. He wasn't just a politician, he was a statesman. And like most of you gathered here there are special thoughts I have in my mind about Harold Washington. Many of you have been encouraged by him. And as his pastor, I feel a great sense of loss. He was my personal friend. I am his pastor. He is my mayor. And he recently became my Frat Brother in Phi Beta Sigma Fraternity. So many good thoughts are in my memory locked. And as every pastor knows, there are some thoughts that must even go to the grave with us. Beyond these persons, however, there are some that I would like to share with you. And I ask your indulgence to listen.

Harold Washington is the compendium of all our historical struggle as Black people in America. He is the apex of all of our present achievement. He is a symbol of all our future aspirations. In a real sense he is the embodiment of our last thirty-three years of Civil Rights gains and progress in America. Caught up in his personage is a vignette ranging from the Dred Scott Decision of 1857, The Brown vs The Board of Education in 1954, The Civil Rights Act of 1964, The Voting Rights Act of 1965, The Fair Housing Amendment of 1968, and all of the subsequent legislation for the enfranchisement of poor and oppressed people in America.

In January of 1987, another star was placed in his crown for his untiring labor to have a day set aside for the celebration of Dr. Martin Luther King, Jr.'s birthday as a national holiday. Harold Washington made good use of the time that God gave him on this earth. It is not how long one lives but how well one lives. Harold lived his life well. He loved life and he lived it fully. Every moment counted for something good and noble for somebody else. He gave all to life and took very little himself. He loved people in general, black, white, yellow, brown and so forth. It didn't matter who you were; and he loved children, especially shy children. If you really want to know what a person is made of watch how he/she treats children. And he made a special place for children on his reform agenda. And I pray to God that it will not fall through the cracks.

He had a special love and concern for senior citizens. And he gave them their respect. He was oftentimes reprimanded by a senior mother. She would say, "you need to sit down to get some rest." He showed special concern for the handicapped and others with disabling conditions. He made things happen in this town. When was it since the last time we have been so inconvenienced trying to get around in the ghetto? Not until Harold Washington began to make things happen for us. A host of economic projects are there to testify to his commitments and loyalty to making those who have been left out included and made to feel a part. Sometimes I wondered what the press would do for news if it wasn't for Harold Washington making things happen in Chicago.

He never forgot people. And I have a case in point. I never will forget his love and concern for a lady by the name of Lois Edwards, his father's secretary and who later became his own secretary. In the sunset of years Harold Washington rose to great power and height in Chicago, but he never forgot Lois. He committed her to the care of the church. Harold had a way, a great capacity to remember the little people, those who were left out, the helpless and the overlooked, Harold Washington remembered.

Also, Harold was full of fun. He had a playful humor about himself. And there was nothing more pleasant than to see that award winning smile flash across his face, to hear him burst forth in laughter.

He could also cut a real bad step on the dance floor. He had an odd singing voice. And he would sing loudly his favorite songs, hymns and ballads. And can't you hear him singing on the last election night the song, "Chicago-Chicago."

Harold also had a toughness about himself. But beneath all that toughness was the real Harold, a compassionate, seriously committed human being. He was warm, gracious and willing to share his all. Harold was a no nonsense person. He didn't have time for foolishness. He didn't have time for inefficiency. And he could not tolerate ineptness at all. He had very little time for ceremony, and I wonder what he would have to say about all of this activity that we are keeping up over him today. He dealt primarily with substantive issues in life, those that went to the heart of causes. He had the best grasp on the principles of cause and effect that I have ever witnessed.

He had a tremendously analytical mind. His mind was like an iron cage. He had very little use for "the finer things of life." Personal material wealth was not a primary focus for his life. Things were not important, but people were vital. He paid little attention to dress codes, social etiquette and other social niceties. His emphasis was always on human relationships and the ethical dynamics that govern those relationships. He was concerned about substance, not style and fashion. Those dynamics of human encounter that make human character whole and complete were his richest values. The love for justice and fairness were important to him. He was concerned about those who were powerless. He was an advocate for those who were poor and weak among us. And for those whose backs were pressed against the wall, Harold always had a word of hope.

Harold was loyal to his friends. Even if such loyalty threatened his well being, he would not forsake a friend. He kept his word. He maintained his integrity.

Harold Washington had a tremendous intellectual capacity, which was also accompanied by a prolific vocabulary with which to express himself. He could speak the Kings English par excellence. So proficient was he in his articulation until all of us, including his constant friends in the media, often had to refer to our dictionaries to find out whether we had been complimented, informed or insulted by his statements. He also had a working knowledge. Not only could he speak the Kings English well, but he had a working knowledge of the Forty-seventh Street black dialect. He knew every idiomatic expression peculiar to the black experience. He could readily communicate his feelings at that level as well. He knew how to talk with black people. He knew how to talk to black people. He knew how to talk about black people. And, he knew how to talk for black people. He never left home.

Harold never left us. He stayed one with us. He never left his real base of support. Harold never abandoned us. And we all knew that Harold, regardless of how long he stayed away, would come home. He loved the third ward, the place of his childhood, his young adulthood and his adult life.

And he was deeply spiritual, not religious. A lot of religious people are going straight to hell. He was deeply spiritual, not sanctimonious. I have been Harold Washington's pastor since 1976. He has been a member of Progressive Community Church since 1982.

His favorite passage of scripture was Psalms 27:103. His favorite song was *If I Can Help Somebody*. He tried hard to make it to church at least once a month, on Communion Sunday. and when he didn't make it, I found my way to his apartment and we had communion. We prayed together at least twice a week. He would always visit other churches, storefronts and cathedrals. No denomination of faith was off limits; he had a ecumenical spirit. No congregation was too small. No pastor was unimportant.

Harold knew the vital importance and the role of the black church in the liberation struggle. He knew the significance of the black church to the life of the movement. He would even go to churches where he was not welcomed.

Harold tried to heal wounds and to bridge the gap that separated Chicago, in terms of racial and ethnic social groups. And I never will forget the stand that he took to keep the storefront churches open. And there was wisdom and understanding in that action. Harold gave his time, his talent and his money to his church. He understood that the church is the only indigenous viable institution in the black community. It needed his support. He surrounded himself early in 1982, and 1983, with spiritual leadership. His campaign was blessed with the prayers of the righteous. His candidacy was anointed for victory by the priests and prophets of the most high God. And his ascendancy to the fifth floor of city hall as Chicago's first black mayor is testimony to the power of God working in the affairs of human events.

His spirituality was expressed in a living commitment. He practiced his faith each day by working to correct wrong doing. He understood that the evils of institutional racism and anti-semitism with their demonic chokehold on lives of the poor, the powerless and disinherited, must be broken. Policies and systems that were nonresponsive and insensitive to human need, he knew it had to be changed. And where there were no policies and no systems to guarantee the delivery of services to people, he worked diligently to shape and form such policies, locally, statewide and nationally. To these ends, Harold Washington dedicated himself.

Now, there is little that we can say or do to add or detract to Harold's record of service. For he alone has so notably lived, served and died that it behooves us just to know that we have stood shoulder to shoulder with such a giant. We have met in this place to affirm his goodness, to thank God for sending him our way, and to commit ourselves to the unfinished agenda of liberation, empowerment and self-determination. We must also commit ourselves to keeping the movement for freedom and justice alive. Harold Washington has done all that he can do to help us. He kept the store well.

He cleaned out the thieves and circumvented the robbers. He left the door of opportunity wide open. And it is up to us to help ourselves and to help others. By his sudden death we have sustained a great wound. We are bleeding; our ship is in troubled waters. The sharks have gotten the scent of our blood. They are after us. We cannot afford to splash about in the water. We must swim or perish. There is no time for power brokering. There is no time for King making. There is no time for ego trips, self serving agendas or hungry power grabs. We must work together in unity of mind and singleness of purpose to keep the spirit of reform alive. My brothers and sisters, the stakes are too high; the causes for which we struggle are much larger than any one man, woman or group.

Too much sacrifice has been made; too much blood, sweat and tears have been shed. We cannot shop now. In the words of the old Civil Rights song, "Ain't gonna let nobody turn me around. We are going to keep on talking. We are going to keep on walking, marching onto freedom's land."

And I have come by here this morning out of the experience of the black ghetto; out of the experience of the black church to say to you in the words of Psalm 27:1, "Except the Lord builds the house, they labor in vain that builded it. Except the Lord keeps the city, the watchman waiteth but in vain." Brothers and sisters we must pray for God's guidance and enlightenment for the challenges that are before us. For no matter how much political conversation we conduct behind closed doors in smoked filled rooms, unless the Lord is invited in our deliberations, unless the spirit of love informs our thoughts, all of our plans are in vain. All of our strategies are like ships without a sail in the midst of a storm at sea. We would be no better than the men and women stumbling around over each other in darkness.

No matter how well trained our staffs are; and no matter how sophisticated our department heads are and no matter how well trained our policemen are, "Except the Lord keeps the city, the watchman waiteth but in vain." We have come a mighty long way by the love and the grace of a good God. Lest we forget, only God will take us through. The God of history. The God who acts through the affairs of men and women. The God who acts in nations, through governments and even through death and tragedy. The God of Abraham, Isaac, Jacob, Sojourner Truth, Harriet Tubman, Frederick Douglass, Malcolm X and Martin Luther King, Jr.; that God. The "I AM THAT I AM, GOD;" the Alpha and Omega, the beginning and the ending. It is our experiences of God that have brought us thus far.

So, we don't come here to mourn or weep. We come here to say let Mount Zion rejoice. And let the daughters of Judea be glad for this God is our God. God is with us.

The road to the future appears to be a rocky road. It is filled with uncertainties, doubts, and anxieties about our common life together as a city, nation and global community. Problems of institutional racism, anti-semitism and unemployment are on the rise. The break down of family life, a troubled educational system, a poorly managed public housing authority, the plight of the homeless, health care, all of which is exasperated by the growing tension in our global order. Our nations involvement in South Africa, the Persian Gulf, South America and in other issues of the Middle East tend to work against world peace. And then if this is not enough, impacting upon these is the frightening reality of a national crisis in leadership.

Confidence in our national leadership is at an all time low. As we watch the Presidential campaign the issues that should dominate the discussion for this high elected office are clouded by selfishness, greed, lasciviousness and false pride. And for us today the lose of a giant like Harold Washington makes it so difficult. Only God can help us through this.

For many people, both black and white these frightening signs of our times sends them into states of paralyzing depression, pessimism, resignation and despair. But for those of us who are of the reformed mind and dare to risk ourselves for the hopes of future generations, these problems are only opportunities for us to strike another blow for freedom. This moment has magic in it.

For here Harold Washington, even in death, has called us to our final summit meeting in this place. He has provided us with great opportunity through his record of service. We have an opportunity to defend ourselves from the evils that nourish injustices and the indifference that tolerates hatred, racial bitterness and the inability to live beyond classism and color. We have an opportunity to teach and encourage our children to fulfill all their potential and promise by showing them by preceipt and example. We must provide for them ample resources to get the job done.

As a religious community, we have an opportunity to make our temples, churches and synagogues to be a living part of God's universal purpose. We must realize that from one blood, God created all nations to dwell upon the face of the earth to prosper and live abundantly in it. We have a golden opportunity to keep our country safe from the ravages of war by electing national leaders equipped with visions, insight and sound judgment. We must work for the peace and justice of all humankind. We must be delivered from the practice of oppression and the conspiracy of power. We must be delivered from the power of violence so that the government of the people, for the people, and by the people should not perish from the earth.

So, let us seize this magic moment as our final salute to our chief. Let us dedicate ourselves to a strong and aggressive reform in the city of Chicago. Let us continue in well doing for there is a great camp meeting in the promised land. Let us work together and pray together. Weep not. Harold Washington is not dead. He lives on beyond the grave. Death does not have the victory. St. Paul says in I Corinthians 15, "For as in Adam all die even so in

Christ shall all be made alive." We do not affirm death but life. We affirm life after life. For Jesus said, "I am the resurrection and the life, though you were dead, yet shall you live. And if you live and believe in me, you shall never die."

Sleep on Harold; go on and take your rest. You labored hard brother. You labored long in the master's vineyard, while it was day. Now that night has come, take your rest. And in the words of Shakespeare's Hamlet, "Good night sweet prince and may flights of angels send thee to thy rest." Let us pick up from where Harold has left off. God bless your hearts. God gives you peace.

Amen.

NOTES ON CONTRIBUTORS

Charles Wesley Jordan is presently serving as Senior pastor of The St. Mark United Methodist Church, Chicago, Illinois. He is formerly District Superintendent in the Southern District, Northern Illinois Conference, United Methodist Church. He received his Master of Divinity degree from Garrett-Evangelical Theological Seminary.

Harry Gibson is presently serving as interim pastor of Gammon United Methodist Church, Chicago, Illinois. He retired recently. His most recent position was Senior Minister of The St. Mark United Methodist Church, Chicago, Illinois. Prior to that he served as an Executive for The Board of Global Ministries, United Methodist Church, New York, City. He is a member of the Norther Illinois Conference of The United Methodist Church. He is a graduate of Philander Smith College and received his Master of Divinity degree from The Interdenominational Theological Seminary, Atlanta, Georgia.

B. Herbert Martin is pastor of Progressive Community Church, Chicago, Illinois. He served as pastor of Harold Washington. He also serves as Chairperson of the Board, Housing Authority, Chicago, Illinois. He is a graduate of Garrett-Evangelical Theological Seminary with a Master of Divinity degree.

Myron McCoy is pastor of South Shore United Methodist Church, Chicago, Illinois. Prior to that appointment he served as Associate minister of St. Mark United Methodist Church, Chicago, Illinois. He serves on the Board of Directors of The Marcy Newbury Center, Chicago, Illinois and Project Image, an organization based at St. Mark United Methodist Church with the commitment to facilitating a positive image on the part of black males in the city of Chicago.

Carroll Felton, Jr. is presently pastor of Kelly United Methodist Church, Chicago, Illinois and a member of The Northern Illinois Annual Conference of The United Methodist Church. He was formerly Director of the Urban Training Center, Chicago, Illinois. He has served on the faculty of The Pittsburgh School of Theology, Pittsburgh, Pennsylvania. He received his Master of Divinity degree from the Interdenominational Theological Center, Atlanta, Georgia.

Albert Sampson holds a Masters degree in Cultural Studies from Governors State University, Park Forest, Illinois and the Masters of Divinity Degree from McCormick Theological Seminary, Hyde Park, Illinois. He was very active in the Civil Rights Movement and worked closely with the late Martin Luther King, Jr. He is presently President of the Council of Black Churches, Pastor of Fernwood United Methodist Church, Chicago, Illinois and served as Vice Chairperson of Mayor Harold Washington's first source task force.

George E. Reddick is Vice President-At-Large of Operation PUSH (People United to Serve Humanity), Chicago, Illinois. He is a frequent lecturer and consultant in church community-based organizations, an ordained Baptist minister and a graduate of The Yale Divinity School, New Haven, Connecticut.

Jeremiah A. Wright, Jr. is pastor of Trinity United Church of Christ, Chicago, Illinois. Trinity is acclaimed as the fastest growing congregation in the United Church of Christ denomination. It is also the largest in membership, having an active membership of 4,500. Jeremiah Wright lectures constantly throughout the country at universities, colleges, seminars and churches on the subject of church growth and evangelism. He holds a Masters degree with a specialization in Phenomenology of Religion from The University of Chicago Divinity School, Chicago, Illinois.

John R. Porter is paster of Christ United Methodist Church, Chicago, Illinois. He holds the Master of Divinity from Garrett-Evangelical Theological Seminary and the Ph.D. from The Graduate Union, Cincinnati, Ohio. He is in increasing demand as a lecturer and consultant. He makes frequent appearances at leading colleges, universities and seminary campuses. He has published a book in the area of Black Youth and Church/Community Development.

Claude S. Wyatt, Jr. is pastor of the Vernon Park Church of God, Chicago, Illinois. He worked closely with the late Martin Luther King, Jr. He assisted King in starting Operation Breadbasket in Chicago, which is presently referred to as Operation PUSH.

Addie S. Wyatt serves as Co-Pastor of Vernon Park Church of God. She has pioneered in establishing the presence of women in ministry as an integral part of the Christian ministry. She worked closely with the late Martin Luther King, Jr. and was instrumental in mobilizing women throughout the Chicago area toward the election and re-election of Harold Washington.

Abraham Patterson Jackson is Pastor of Liberty Baptist Church, Chicago, Illinois. He is a graduate of Morehouse College, Atlanta, Georgia, where he was one of Benjamin Elijah May's first students. He received the Masters of Divinity Degree from Garrett-Evangelical Theological Seminary. Because of his involvement in the Civil Rights struggle and close working relationship with Martin Luther King, Jr., Liberty Baptist was selected by King as his headquarters whenever he came to Chicago.

Darrell Lamar Jackson, the son of Abraham Patterson Jackson, is also a graduate of Morehouse College and holds the Masters of Divinity degree from Garrett-Evangelical Theological Seminary. He serves on the ministerial staff of Liberty Baptist Church, Chicago, Illinois.

Hycel Taylor is Pastor of Second Baptist Church, Chicago, Illinois. He holds the Doctor of Ministry degree from Vanderbilt Divinity

School, Nashville, Tennessee. He formerly served as Director of The Church and the Black Experience and Professor of Applied Theology at Garrett-Evangelical Theological Seminary. He also served as Executive Director of Operation PUSH, Chicago, Illinois.

Sylvester Brinson, III is Pastor of Hope Tabernacle Assembly of God, Chicago, Illinois. He is a graduate of Garrett-Evangelical Theological Seminary with the Masters of Divinity Degree. He is presently a candidate for the Doctor of Ministry Degree at Trinity Evangelical Seminary, Deerfield, Illinois.

Jesse Cotton was serving as Pastor of the Greater Institutional African Methodist Episcopal Church, Chicago, Illinois, during the time of Harold Washington's Administration. He is presently serving Community African Methodist Church, Grand Rapids, Michigan. During his entire administration, Harold Washington relied very heavily on council and support from Jesse Cotton.

Wilfred Reid is Paster of Grant Memorial African Methodist Episcopal Church, Chicago, Illinois. Prior to coming to Grant, he served as Pastor of St. Stephen A.M.E. Church, Chicago. He holds the Masters of Divinity degree and has done work toward the Doctor of Ministry degree at Garrett-Evangelical Theological Seminary.

John Parker is Pastor of New Life Baptist Church, Chicago, Illinois. He is very involved in social activism and worked untiringly in the Harold Washington political campaign.

Eugene Gibson is Pastor of the Mission of Faith Baptist Church, Chicago. He holds several academic degrees including a Doctorate in Theology. He serves as a consultant in Christian Education for the Southern Baptist Convention. He is a frequent lecturer in Christian Education for various church groups throughout the country.

George Walker serves as Pastor of the Greater African Methodist Episcopal Zion Church, Chicago, Illinois. He is a graduate of Livestone College, Hood Theological Seminary and holds an honorary Doctorate degree. He is in increasing demand as a preacher through his denominational network.

Nathaniel Jarrett is Pastor of Martin Temple African Methodist Episcopal Zion Church, Chicago, Illinois. He holds the Master of Divinity degree from the Yale Divinity School, New Haven, Connecticut and the Doctor of Ministry degree from The Chicago Theological Seminary, Chicago, Illinois. He serves on many boards and agencies throughout the Chicago area, including Vice President of Project Image.

Charles Murray serves as Pastor of New Galilee Missionary Baptist Church, Chicago, Illinois. He attended Moody Bible Institute and the Chicago Baptist Institute.

Marvell Williams is Pastor of The New Mount Moriah Missionary Baptist Church, Chicago, Illinois. He attended Mississippi State University, Chicago Baptist Institute and Malcolm X Junior College.

Brenda Little received a Master of Divinity Degree in Pastoral Ministry and Counseling from Northern Baptist Theological Seminary, Lombard, Illinois in 1979. She holds a Bachelor of Religion Education Degree from Chicago Baptist Institute; graduating in 1976. She has done post-graduate work at both Garrett-Evangelical Seminary Northern Baptist Theological Seminary with a major in Parish or Congregational Ministry. She is now a candidate for the Doctorate of Ministry Degree.

David C. Coleman is presently a Presiding Elder in The African Methodist Episcopal Church, Chicago Area. He formerly served as Pastor of Bethel African Methodist Episcopal Church, Chicago, Illinois. He holds degrees from The University of Arizona, Tucson, Arizona and the Masters of Divinity from Payne Theological Seminary, Zenia, Ohio.

Willie Barrow served as a Delegate to the 1984 National Democratic Convention; member of the Executive Committee to Elect Harold Washington, Mayor of Chicago; appointed by Governor James Thompson to The Illinois Council to make January 15 a State Holiday commemorating the birthday of Dr. Martin Luther King, Jr. She is currently the National Executive Director of Operation PUSH, a National Board Member of the National Political Congress of Black Women, Honorary Member of Sigma Gamma Rho Sorority, and was named by *Dollars and Sense* Magazine as one of the "100 Top Black Business and Professional Women." She and her husband Claude, a native of British Honduras, reside in the South Shore community of Chicago and she serves as an Associate Minister and Trustee of the Vernon Park Church of God.

Henry O. Hardy has just celebrated his 20th year as Pastor of Cosmopolitan Community Church in Chicago. A graduate of the University of Illinois School of Journalism, Hardy received the Bachelor of Divinity from the Divinity School of the University of Chicago. He also earned a Masters of Art Degree in Theology and Literary Criticism from the University of Chicago. A gifted writer and poet, Rev. Mr. Hardy is a former journalist who has written for the *St. Louis Argus, Chicago Defender* and *Gary American* newspapers. While a student at the University of Illinois, he published in the *Crisis* magazine.

Clay Evans was ordained as a Baptist Minister in 1950; founder and pastor of Fellowship Missionary Baptist Church - Chicago for thirty-seven years. He is an alumnus of the following schools: Carver High School, Brownsville, Tennessee, Chicago Baptist Institute, Northern Baptist Theological Seminary, The University of Chicago Divinity School, Cortez Peters Business College, Trinity College and the International Bible Institute and Seminary from which he received the Bachelor and Master Degrees in Ministry. Pastor Evans received honorary Doctor of Divinity Degrees from Arkansas Baptist College and Brewster Theological Clinic and School of Religion.

Clarence Hilliard is Pastor of Austin Corinthian Baptist Church, Chicago, Illinois. He holds a degree from Houghton College and has done graduate work at Trinity Seminary, Deerfield, Illinois. Some of the other professional responsibilities include: Developer and Instructor of course for Trinity Seminary, Deerfield, Illinois (Summer Inner-city Seminary, Pt 602 and Pt 603) 1970-71 Ministry, Step (church renewal organization) 1973-76 Teacher, Lecturer, Workshop and Seminar Leader for college, university and seminary students, ministers and laypersons.

Eddie L. Robinson has been appointed pastor of Delaney Memorial United Methodist Church in Gary, Indiana. The appointment is effective June 1. Since 1981, he has been editor of promotional materials for United Methodist Communications' Evanston-based Division of Program and Benevolence Interpretation. In his current position he is responsible for developing and producing printed and audiovisual resources to interpret The United Methodist Church's $6.3 million Missional Priority Fund. A long-time Chicago-area resident, Mr. Robinson attended school there, receiving an Associate in Arts degree from Wilson Jr. College, part of the Chicago City College system. He also holds a Bachelor of Arts degree from Goshen (Ind.) College and a Master of Divinity degree from Garrett-Evangelical Theological Seminary in Evanston, Illinois.

Willie Upshire is Pastor of The Prince of Peace Missionary Baptist Church, Chicago, Illinois.. He attended McKinley Theological Seminary at Jackson, Mississippi where he received a B.A. degree in Humanities, a B.A. in Social Science and a Doctorate of Divinity, graduating in May of 1977. He also has attended the Illinois School of Law and graduated in March, 1981.